Grant MacEwan's Journals

Edited by Max Foran

Assisted by Judy Dundas

Preface by Hugh Dempsey

The Publishers:
Lone Pine Publishing
414, 10357 109 Street
Edmonton, Alberta
T5J 1N3

Typesetting by Pièce de Résistance Typographers, Edmonton

Printed and Bound in Canada by D.W. Friesen & Sons Ltd., Altona, Manitoba

Canadian Cataloguing in Publication Data

MacEwan, Grant, 1902-
    Grant MacEwan's journals

ISBN 0-919433-07-3

    1. MacEwan, Grant, 1902-   2. Lieutenant-governors—Alberta—Biography.*
3. Historians—Prairie Provinces—Biography. 4. Agriculturists—Prairie
Provinces—Biography. 5. Politicians—Prairie Provinces—Biography. I. Foran,
Max. II. Title.
FC3675.1.M234A3 1985   971.2'009'94   C85-091610-0
F1078.M234A3 1985

All photos courtesy the MacEwan family except where noted.

Contents

Acknowledgements

First and foremost, I would like to thank Grant MacEwan for allowing me to edit his personal journals for publication, and for his help and co-operation in providing elaboration and other relevant details.

My deep debt of appreciation is acknowledged to Judy Dundas for her invaluable aid in the whole editing process, and to Joe Dundas for helping to facilitate the final preparation of the manuscript.

A special note of thanks is reserved for Deirdre Slater and Elaine Edwards for their sterling efforts in typing the manuscript.

Finally, I would like to thank my wife Heather, whose suggestion it was that this fascinating historical record be edited and shared with the public.

Max Foran
Priddis, Alberta
February 1986

Preface
by Hugh Dempsey

Some men, if they are well organized, can wear two hats at the same time; some might even manage three or four. But there are few who could match Grant MacEwan and the vast array of headgear he has donned over the years. Author, politician, historian, agriculturist, lecturer, mayor of Calgary, Lieutenant-Governor of Alberta—each has provided him with a separate career and each had been handled with deftness and skill.

There are some interesting statistics about Grant MacEwan—even if they tell only part of the story. For example, he has written 32 books, more than 2,500 newspaper columns, and delivered more than 6,000 speeches, lectures, and radio addresses. And that's only the literary part of his career.

Born in Manitoba in 1902, he was raised in Melfort, Saskatchewan, and educated at the Ontario College of Agriculture and the University of Iowa. In his professional career, he was on the staff of the University of Saskatchewan, Dean of Agriculture at the University of Manitoba, Alderman and then Mayor of Calgary, a Member of the Alberta Legislative Assembly, and Lieutenant-Governor of Alberta. In his spare time he has lectured, written books and articles, judged livestock shows, and served on innumerable boards and commissions.

There are many examples of his prowess in each of his chosen fields. For example, at a banquet sponsored by an international group in Calgary, a couple of members were heard to say they were going to slip away during the after-dinner speech of the Lieutenant-Governor because it would probably be dull and parochial. When Grant MacEwan had finished, the men were still there, sides sore from laughing, hands tingling from clapping, and their minds enlivened and enlightened from what they had heard. It hadn't been a speech but a combination of story-telling, hard facts, and humour all skillfully entwined.

On another occasion the archives of the Glenbow Museum suddenly became crowded with young people. They were students from Grant MacEwan's university class who were so inspired by his lectures that they had come to seek original

5

documents and papers on the history of the West. It takes a special kind of teacher to arouse this type of enthusiasm.

The many stories about Grant MacEwan are as interesting and varied as the ones he recounts about his heroes from the past. Academics speak fondly of his habit of avoiding unnecessary waste by travelling by bus and staying at the local YMCA when on research trips. This same man reflected the independent attitude of pioneers when he built his own log cabin in the foothills when most people his age had given up such exertions. And while the Lieutenant-Governor, then a man in his sixties, he wore out young reporters who tried to interview him while he was jogging.

But behind the veneer of a lovable, folksy westerner stands a resolute man. Well-organized and well-disciplined, he can be forceful and unyielding when facing issues which question the traditional ethics of hard work, honesty, and service to his fellow man. He expects much of himself but he also expects something from society.

There is no room in his life for the dilettante or the shirker. The early West was made up of independent and industrious men, like those discussed in his volume *Fifty Mighty Men* (Saskatoon: Modern Press, 1958). And standing with them were the pioneer women, like the ones who appeared in his companion volume . . . *And Mighty Women Too* (Saskatoon: Prairie Books, 1975). Grant MacEwan has followed their principles of hard work and service throughout his life and has seen no reason to move away from those standards which created an agricultural and industrial West.

This philosophy is clearly reflected in his book *Entrusted To My Care* (Saskatoon: Modern Press, 1966) where he states: "As I grow older, I become more and more convinced that I could serve no finer moral purpose than to make myself a guardian of the good gifts of Nature." This service that he has performed is not for his own fame or well being, but to the land and its people. And in achieving that objective, he has given something to all of us. At the same time, almost inadvertently, he has placed his own name in the annals of history just as surely as he has preserved the names of others.

Hugh A. Dempsey
Curator
Glenbow Museum
Calgary

Editor's Foreword
by Max Foran

My association with Grant MacEwan dates to 1963 when I arrived in Canada from Australia to marry his daughter, Heather. As his son-in-law and friend, I have come to know, respect and most of all, learn from him. Our mutual interest in history and writing has meant many discussions and exchanges of ideas, which have resulted in my fuller understanding of his attitudes, values and overall philosophy. Over the years I have exhorted him to write his autobiography knowing full well that it was not in his nature to do so. Grant MacEwan genuinely believes that his own life and accomplishments are scarcely worth a personal reminiscence, let alone the overstatement of an autobiography.

He agreed, however, to my editing his personal journals for publication. But in my capacity as editor I have done more than just edit. I have tried in my selection of entries, to give readers a clearer picture of the man himself as well as the events which have marked his life to 1965. Also, many of my own comments are interpretive as well as explanatory. Readers should be aware of this editorial licence as they make their way through these fascinating first-hand comments. For while the journals are Grant MacEwan's, the testimonial is my own.

Max Foran
October 1985

Grant MacEwan on his father's shoulder, 1904

MacEwan Roots
by Maria Nelson

The man who walked so many hundreds of miles in marches to support a variety of worthy causes during his term as the Queen's representative in Alberta, John Walter Grant MacEwan has had from his earliest years a lively curiosity and an active mind which prompted a growing interest in the wonders of the world around him.

Although Grant has always had a delightful sense of humour, and during his university years was a keen athlete (playing football and basketball with distinction at Guelph), he was motivated by a strong sense of self-discipline and a conviction, even as a young man, that he owed something to the good land on which he lived.

Even now that he has reached 80 years of age, he chops his wood for his fireplace, he fells trees with a handsaw, builds log cabins, walks and hikes miles, and rides unbroken horses. When one hears of this prowess the question arises: "What is the source of all this vigour and enthusiasm?" Let us look at his roots. The doctors tell us that the best prescription for a long and healthy life is the wise choice of healthy grandparents.

On both sides of Grant MacEwan's family, he comes from an unadulterated Scottish line. His grandfather, George MacEwan, came to Canada from Stirling, Scotland, in 1850. He settled in Guelph, Ontario, where he practised as a blacksmith. Later, he became an engineer with the Raymond Sewing Machine Company, where he worked for 30 years.

Shortly after George arrived in Canada, he met a pretty Scottish lass, Annie Cowan. They were married and raised their family in Guelph. It was here that their first son, Alexander, was born. Growing up as he did in a beautiful agricultural area, Alec developed a passion for good horses. A boyhood dream was to go to Montana and become a cowboy. That dream never left him, and eventually as a young man he set out for the west on the new Canadian Pacific Railway. He reached Brandon, Manitoba, where on impulse he hopped off the train to see the country. It may very well have been during harvest, one of the loveliest seasons in the west. Finding employment was no problem in those days— Alec quickly found a job north of Brandon. He liked the country so well that he decided to stay, and before many months, he had acquired a farm of his own and a fine team of horses.

One of Alec MacEwan's neighbours, James Grant, was an immigrant from Nova Scotia, who took an interest in this eager, hard-working young man. Grant was especially impressed by MacEwan's skill with and knowledge of fine horses. The neighbourhood assessment was no doubt, ''Here is a young man with fine prospects!''

James Grant had a sister, Bertha, who had come out west from Pictou County to join the first nurses' training class at the Brandon General Hospital. Grant arranged to have his sister and Alec MacEwan meet. James Grant always claimed that he was the guiding light who lit the flame of that romance. The young couple were married the year after Bertha graduated from the hospital, and they established their first home on Alec MacEwan's homestead.

Their son Grant, born in August 1902, was named for his maternal grandfather, John Walter Grant. J.W. Grant's great-grandfather, James Grant, had come from the Highlands of Scotland to Pictou Harbour on a sailing ship in 1773. J.W. Grant MacEwan is therefore a sixth generation Highland Canadian.

Maria Nelson is Grant MacEwan's first cousin and oldest surviving relative.

Grant MacEwan: An Overview
by Max Foran

Grant MacEwan is truly one of western Canada's most identifiable figures. He has lived for extended periods of time in all three prairie provinces and has come to know them and their people in a way difficult to emulate. He has studied and written about their histories and their heroes in over 30 published works. He has had an intimate association with the land itself, first as a farm youngster, then as a professional agriculturist, and lately as a champion of conservation. His role as a public figure has enabled him to touch the lives of his fellow westerners in unique and lasting ways. The many talents and abilities of this remarkably versatile man are fleshed out solidly in Rusty Macdonald's biography, aptly entitled *No Ordinary Man* (Western Producer, 1979). This is fortunate, since MacEwan makes little reference in his diaries to his own accomplishments. What does emerge from these diaries are three dominant characteristics, all of which are useful to a fuller understanding of this unassuming, yet strangely complex individual.

First, there is Grant MacEwan's commitment to public life. From the day he assumed his teaching position at the University of Saskatchewan in 1928, he put his duties to his profession and to the agricultural community above all else. Political activities in the 1940's, 1950's and 1960's, plus growing celebrity status, resulted in the emergence of a public figure writ large. MacEwan's total commitment to public life and his ability to handle its demands with amazing consistency and unimpeachable integrity have served to blur the private person beneath. Indeed, after a lifetime of service to the public, the private Grant MacEwan is rarely revealed. The diaries unfold a litany of public deeds without much of a hint as to the private thoughts of the man who performed them.

Second, is MacEwan's obsession with the work ethic. Even by workaholic standards he is extreme. His relentless regimen of task completion has produced prodigious results as well as a legion of personal anecdotes. It has also meant an increasing inability to relax and a steady withdrawal from the world of sustained social dialogue and personal intimacies. In short, MacEwan assesses his priorities solely in terms of jobs to be done. All else must be either shelved or fitted fleetingly in between tasks. The diaries are very illuminative here, for they document this addiction to work from its very early manifestation as a youngster.

Finally, and probably most importantly from MacEwan's viewpoint, has been his gradual disenchantment with the Judeo-Christian tradition which emphasizes Man's special relationship with God. It took MacEwan many years to come to his current belief that God is in all things in nature, and that Man is at best just another participant, but more often than not a rapacious disturber of the natural order. The diaries are illuminative for they show MacEwan's early orthodoxy, while making reference to a change in direction as early as the 1930's. However, it is the book's final section which best shows the extent of this transition.

MacEwan's commitment to public life and the work ethic, plus his adoption of religious universalism, have largely shaped his actions. Together they explain his gregariousness and good humour, his indifference to personal or social frivolities, his absorption with work, his concern for the land and its creatures, his need to conserve, and above all, that enigmatic quality recognizable by those closely associated with him. The diaries highlight all these qualities except the enigmatic, which fortunately receives some qualification in the interview. Taken together, the diaries and the interview offer a first-person commentary on the development of Grant MacEwan's life, career and philosophy. And since he will not write his autobiography, this is as much as his countless admirers can ever hope for.

Reflections as a Boy
1914-1921

The urge to commit life's events to paper has been a part of Grant MacEwan for as long as he can remember. In the beginning, he used scraps of paper or small pocket-books filled with childish scrawl and poor spelling. Later, in the 1920's and again in the 1930's, he revised these original notes into a more permanent journal record. Thus, this first selection of entries covering his early life up to the end of 1921, is somewhat reflective and written in prose more mature than normally expected from a youngster.

The journals themselves deserve some elaboration. There are three, two of which are hard-bound and cover 302 and 256 pages respectively. MacEwan's frugal writing is small and compact and not always easily decipherable. While entries appear regularly, they were not made on a daily basis. Generally, the right-hand pages were used for formal, dated entries, with the left-hand side reserved for extraneous material such as letters, clippings and anecdotal accounts. The two journals, therefore, present a wider scope than that provided by the diary extracts which comprise this volume. The newspaper clippings, for example, document MacEwan's growing public stature, while his letters show his strong emotional attachment to his parents.

The third book covers his career from 1958 to 1965 and is much smaller, not containing the extraneous material of the first two. Mainly it is concerned with his political experiences as leader of the Alberta Liberal Party in the elections of 1959, and his mayoralty term in Calgary, 1964-65.

These journals offer little in the way of self-analysis or critical commentary. They do, however, show the development of a remarkable individual through time and experience. In this respect, they resemble their author. They speak in the same light-hearted, yet straightforward manner that has endeared Grant MacEwan to three generations of Western Canadians.

It is difficult to imagine Grant MacEwan as a boy. While he remained young at heart, there was not the caprice, mischievousness and dependency normally associated with childhood. Instead, his early diary entries note the same personal qualities that later were associated with him as a man. This boy, who was never really a boy, was energetic, thrifty and knew the value of a dollar. He was involved in worthwhile projects and, even in these early writings, showed that he could see the funny side of life.

His diary opens in Brandon, Manitoba around 1914. There the MacEwan family lived, having moved from the farm some years earlier to start a fire extinguisher business. Typically, his opening entries show him making a dollar.

c. 1913 - 1914   There was always some business afoot. For several years I had a newspaper route and served the *Brandon Sun* for the sum of $1.50 a week. There were other odd jobs that a mercenary boy could find delight in. I sold vegetables nearly all summer and, what was particularly remunerative, the sale of mushrooms. A few of these lowly plants grew on our lot, but other carefully guarded beds were located and visited with maximum secrecy.

Brandon summer fairs offered money-making possibilities. One year I sold cigars, peanuts, gum, chocolate bars, etc. on a 20% commission. That meant "big money." I could get into the fair grounds by jumping the fence on the north side and as I carried all my wares I paid no concession duty. It was a great business. There was one sad mishap when I was trying to make sales in a crowd that was watching the Traveller's Parade. As I pushed through the crowd, glancing now and again at the parade, I tripped and let all my valuable wares—cigars, gum and candy—scatter on the ground and among the feet of the people about me.

It was my ambition, much more than that of other boys, to make money. A school savings account was opened when in my second grade, and weekly deposits were made. Expenditures thereafter, as before, were nil.

July 1, 1914   With the beginning of holidays, I set out to find summer employment. I secured a job as clerk and errand boy for George Fitton, grocer on 14th Street. I began at 8:00 a.m. and worked until 6:30 p.m., 10:30 p.m. on Saturdays, for $3.00 a week. It gave me a little money, considerable experience and a wealth of satisfaction. It was during my employment with Fitton's Grocery that World War I broke out. From August 4, 1914, when Great Britain declared war on Germany, it was part of my noon hour duties to take Fitton's money to the bank on my father's bicycle, then swing around to the *Brandon Sun's* bulletin board and get the latest war news. Before the summer months were expired, I was not only banking the boss's money, but was frequently left in charge of the store.

I always had an abnormal respect for a dollar. A dollar earned meant a dollar saved and never throughout public school years was as much as five cents spent at one time on candies. I could at times be persuaded to part with one cent for candies, but never more.

MacEwan's father, Alexander, was a tough Ontarian of Scottish descent who had come west to Brandon in 1889. He married Bertha Grant, a nurse, in 1900. Bertha's two brothers, Jim and John, also farmed in the Brandon district. The Grants were a proud family with roots in Canada dating back to 1773, when the ship, *Hector*, carried James Grant to Pictou County, Nova Scotia.

Grant MacEwan, or more properly, John Walter Grant MacEwan, was born on August 12, 1902. His brother, George, was born five years later. Bertha MacEwan was a staunch Presbyterian, and determined that her children should receive a good solid background in the church.

c. 1915 The church and its organizations loomed large in my early life. For years I had a perfect attendance at Knox Presbyterian Church Sunday School. I belonged to Knox Mission Band and was active in all its undertakings. At our departure from Brandon, I was a recipient of the book, "Souls in Action," as a parting gift from Mrs. F. McKenzie, President, and Knox Church Mission Band, dated April 13, 1915.

MacEwan's love of music, and in particular the bagpipes, is well known to his friends. His musical ability, however, falls far short of his aspirations as shown by the following.

c. 1915 The account of Brandon school-days would not be complete without some reference to the Alexander School orchestra. Mr. Hunter, the principal, was the sponsor and, being quite without understanding of such things, I aspired to be a part of it. I received no encouragement from my father, who had his own ideas about making musicians of boys, but I secured a catalogue of musical instruments and studied it with the greatest of thought. I wanted a coronet or a trombone, but their costs were prohibitive. There was only one instrument that would fit my appropriation, and that was a B-flat flute, priced at $5.00. I got it and practised religiously for two years, and eventually decided that I was not musical, that the flute was no good, and that the orchestra was no place for me.

Given his background, it is not surprising to find that farming greatly appealed to young MacEwan. But farming was not something he dreamed about; it was something that needed immediate attention.

c. 1915 From the age of 12 years on, my ambition was to farm and raise good livestock. The proposal that the family would go back to the farm met with the heartiest welcome, and I for one was prepared to cooperate. I attended the public auction sales at the city market and with the few cents entrusted to my care I, on one occasion, bought a serviceable pick for 30 cents and on another occasion, a hand scythe for 40 cents. They formed the nucleus of our farm equipment.

It was in 1913, at the age of ten years, that I bought my first bovine. The purchase of a calf for $2.00 was made without the consent of my parents and I was not permitted to keep it. It turned out all right, however, because I was able to sell the animal for $3.00, thus making a clear dollar on the deal.

In April, 1916, when we had been one year at Melfort and aspiring to own a herd of cattle, an arrangement between my father and me was entered into, and by it I was to pay $50 (most of the savings I had after carefully guarding every nickel I made for several years) and he to pay the balance, namely $30 toward the purchase of the Holstein cow, "Spot." I was to own all her calves and he was to get all the milk. The deal seemed quite promising until Spot calved a dead calf in May of that year. She failed to get in calf again and the cow was eventually salvaged to the butcher, and I recovered only a fraction of my investment. The cow was a record milker and gave 100 pounds a day on three times a day milking for a period in June.

My next investment was $30 in a calf which had had a touch of rickets, but was otherwise a beautiful calf. It was only on the farm a few weeks, however, until it strayed off into a bluff one day and died from black-leg.

Then I purchased a cow with calf at foot from Malcolm McPhail for $100. The calf looked like a prospective show animal, but it was so wild all its life that it could not be fattened. It was a source of worry and trouble. The cow was bred again, but died calving the next spring with a useless veterinary man looking at her and aggravating her trouble, all the while anticipating the collection of $10 which he fully realized, but certainly did not earn.

At another time, a red cow in calf to our own Angus bull was bought from Ted Frank. She calved a nice black bull calf that was fattened successfully.

It was this promising calf that my brother and I entered into a partnership on, for the purposes of making a show steer. Among other incidents in connection with the feeding of that calf, was the time we wanted some molasses to make his ration complete. I agreed to remain at home while George went to town to buy the three gallons of molasses. His instructions were to secure Can Mola (a then-popular brand of feeding molasses) from A.E. Code. The boy was strange in town and became a bit confused. He went to Codes all right, asked for three gallons of Coca Cola. He was advised by Mr. Code that he would have to go to Graham's Confectionery to get Coca Cola. The innocent kid journeyed to the confectionary, but this time asked for three gallons of Cane Mola, and was again told he must get it elsewhere—probably at Codes. He went back to Codes again and asked for Coca Cola, then came home in disgust.

Caught in the pre-war economic collapse, Alexander MacEwan was forced to liquidate his business. In 1915, he set off with young Grant for Margo, Saskatchewan to begin farming on land he had bought sight unseen some time earlier. Finding that they had been grossly misled and that the land at Margo was woefully inadequate, father and son headed for Melfort, Saskatchewan to view a section purchased in 1906. MacEwan details the journey west and the beginnings of a new life.

Spring, 1915 My father's business enterprises less profitable than anticipated. Hard times for the family. Decided to go back to the land. My father traded some of his numerous and unprofitable parcels of city real estate on five quarters of land at Margo, Saskatchewan and it was to that point we proposed to go. Two old plugs of horses were bought at $50 each and they, along with old Polly, the Jersey cow, about 25 hens and our household belongings, were placed in a freight car for shipment to our new home. The only two suggestions of farm machinery in the car were the scythe and pick which I had purchased at the city square for a total of 70 cents, and the old family lawn mower.

April 17, 1915 My father and I left Brandon on a C.N.R. freight with a car of effects billed for Margo. Our trip was very interesting because I was a stow-away and must keep under cover. On one occasion I was in my hiding place and while Dad was out in the town to get some bread, one of the train crew came in, stole one of our best hens, and I was obliged to view the event in silence.

April 20, 1915 Arrived at Margo. The first day was devoted to the unloading of our car and the making of some contacts in the village. Mr. De Galliers and old Mr. Chapman were helpful and interesting acquaintances. I investigated public school facilities because I was anxious to complete public schooling that season. The boys around town wanted a catcher for their baseball team and hoped that I would stay with them.

April 21, 1915 The day was rainy, but we hitched our two horses to a borrowed wagon, piled it high with furniture and effects, tied old Polly behind and started off to locate our 800 acre farm which neither of us had ever seen. We found the farm, but not as represented. The land was not as described, the cultivated acreage was not ready for crop, the buildings were quite unsatisfactory and without unloading our effects or unharnessing the team, my father, upon whom the responsibility of decisions evolved, decided to drive back to Margo and plan another course. After one hour on the farm we turned back in the rain, reloaded our car and billed for Melfort.

April 22, 1915 We were on our way to Melfort, via Prince Albert. Our hopes were now directed toward a piece of land—one section (23-44-19-2) in the Melfort district. This parcel of unimproved land was bought in 1906 for purely speculative purposes, but a kind providence prevented the resale.

My father and I lived for the week in which we were travelling, on bread, Polly's milk and 25 cents worth of fancy biscuits.

April 24, 1915 Arrived Melfort. It was a bustling little town in those days. One week since we left Brandon.

Two boys, looking for trouble, lit cigarettes and throwing a lighted match into our car, fired the hay which I extinguished with considerable difficulty.

April 25, 1915 Sunday, Dad and I went out (Dad on foot and I on a bicycle) to see the farm. It didn't look very promising to me. There was no fence, no house, no cultivation, but abundance of trees. We camped that night and for two nights following, at Sparrow's barn at the east of town where we were permitted to store some of our belongings.

April 27, 1915   Drove out to the farm with a load of furniture and the old cow. We pulled in at the bluff just off the trail to make a temporary camp. There we stayed and there we later erected the farm buildings.

April 28, 1915   Mother and George, who were wired to remain in Brandon for a few weeks, ignored instructions, came on, and arrived. We all spent the night in I. Poole's granary where some of our belongings were stored.

April 29, 1915   Jas. Durnin, farmer on the south of us, agreed to let us use his old bed-bug infested, log building which was in use as a granary. We used it for sleeping quarters and by day lived in an enclosure made by crated furniture in the bluff. I will never forget how acceptable was the first mess of boiled potatoes we cooked over an open fire beside the bluff.

April 30, 1915   Money was a scarce article. My father had about $50 when he arrived and most of that amount was spent on a second-hand wagon that served us well. Certain expenditures were absolutely necessary. My sire was able to place a mortgage ($3,000) on the land and thereby secure some funds with which to work.

May 3, 1915   We purchased a one-roomed shack, 16'x18', in the town and this we moved onto the farm. It seemed splendid to be once more living under our own roof.

The day of moving the house to the farm was a long one. Dad and I, with two sets of wagon gear (one a borrowed one) and two horses, made the move. We had the house within two miles of home by darkness that night. The noon-day meal that day cost us a total of 5 cents each, and consisted of eight buns which I purchased in town at 15 cents a dozen.

May 8, 1915   Began to construct the stable. The stable was built from poles cut on the farm, and about $100 worth of shiplap.

May 10, 1915   George and I started to Spry School. My shoes, a pair of patent leather button boots previously worn by the widely known Dare Devil Blakely, who had the year before flown an aeroplane at the Brandon Exhibition and left two pair of stylish boots behind, cut a wide swath. I hardly knew whether to be proud or ashamed of them.

Miss Olive Durnin was the teacher. It was so close to the end of the term and work so different from that of Manitoba, that I was forced to drop back to Grade 7, a grade which I had never taken.

We walked to and from school and carried our dinners which consisted quite consistently of egg sandwiches, and mighty good ones they were. For preparing simple, wholesome and palatable food, my mother had never been excelled.

Editor's Note: The first example of MacEwan's latent leadership qualities occurred at school when he acted as the spokesman to protest an inappropriate class project.

June 25, 1915   A difficulty at school. The teacher proposed that some time be devoted to raffia work in school and that each pupil bring 50 cents for the purchase of materials. That was a large sum to we boys. We talked it over at home and the next day when the matter was again under discussion in school, I took the bit in my teeth, arose in my seat and explained to teacher and all that the money would only be secured with difficulty in our home and perhaps others, and it would be more satisfactory for us if the time were devoted to something less costly—I suggested physical training or something equally novel. The raffia work was never started.

December 12, 1915 Mother and George and I left for Brandon. Our accommodation at the farm was hardly suitable and we were invited to live with Uncle Jim Grant for the winter—Mother to take care of the house in Aunt Marion's absence in the east.

December 31, 1915 Miss Durnin of Spry School kindly agreed to send me the Christmas exams and with more than average confidence in a pupil, left it to myself to write the papers and keep my own time, etc. I was high in the class.

At Melfort the MacEwan boys continued their church-going ways under the guidance of Bertha. This time however their (or Bertha's) faith was tested more rigorously.

July 11, 1915 Mother and George and I attended St. James Church in Melfort with fair regularity. It was a strenuous trip on foot. We would have to leave home about 9:30 or 9:45, and if we stayed for Sunday School which followed church service at 12 o'clock, we would not be home until 2:30 p.m. By that time we were ravenous for food.

It meant something to have a mother whose faith was as firm as Gibraltar and who thought sufficient of her God and her church that she, with her two boys, would walk 8 1/2 miles, in addition to her regular housework, that the benefits of church service would arise.

In the fall of 1917 after a hard summer's work on the farm, which was four miles from Melfort, Alexander MacEwan and Grant built their first home at Melfort. Grant often said in later life, when asked about his exceptional building ability, that he just learned by doing.

May, 1917 The crop in; we prepared to do more breaking. We had five horses in that season and my father and I worked together all summer. Feed was scarce so we made only seven or eight miles per half day with the teams (two drivers and one plow) and utilized all the spare moments cutting and grubbing along our lands. The flies were nothing short of terrible that season and the heat too was painful at times. We broke 35 acres on the south quarters. The 15 acre field was broken and the first breaking was done on the east side of the southwest quarter (20 acres).

August, 1917 Purchased a new Froste and Wood binder from Jack Stewart, dealer, Melfort. Dad drove the binder. I did most of the stooking.

September 14, 1917 Again, Rod Reid did our threshing with his old Case steam outfit.

September, 1917 Threshing completed, we decided to build a more suitable house for ourselves. The decision was made rather suddenly and the work commenced so soon after, that little planning was done.

My father and I excavated a basement but the season was advanced and funds limited, so we decided that no foundation would be put in at that time. The house was started about October 1 and built on blocks. The house was 30' x 30' with a kitchen 12' x 16' in addition.

November 25, 1917 We moved into our new shell of a house. It was foundationless, plasterless, and lacked the finished flooring, but it looked like a million dollars to us.

Over the years, Grant MacEwan was to mention often a speech he had heard in 1918 by Dean W.J. Rutherford, President of the University of Saskatchewan. MacEwan was in Regina at the time with the five-boy Melfort team competing in the annual Farm Boys' Camp. In the following extract, he refers to both the camp and to Rutherford's address.

July 30 to August 2, 1918 We were quartered at Connaught School in Regina and the competitions, for the most part, were held at the exhibition grounds.

Military movements were the order of the day and the poor farm boys were drilled and marched beyond all reason.

I scored high in one competition and near the top in others.

On the last day of the fair, we as a group visited the legislative buildings. It was assembled in those buildings that I first saw and heard Dean W.J. Rutherford of Saskatoon. He talked for a few minutes on a topic I have forgotten. A lot of water has passed under the bridge and a lot of topics and addresses have been heard and forgotten, but Dean Rutherford's text lingers green within my memory. It has lost none of its value and loftiness in the years. Few texts could be found more suitable for a talk to a bunch of boys and indeed I have used it myself a few times. It was this, "*The boy increased in wisdom and in stature; and in favor with God and man.*"

Stories about MacEwan's physical stamina are legion. He exhibited it at an early age judging by the following account.

March 31, 1920 A very bad storm all day. Mother, as well as Dad, is down with flu today and Dad's headache powders were exhausted. The poor man was frantic. I tried to drive a horse to town for a fresh supply, but the brute would scarcely face the storm, so I did the only other thing; I walked in and back and waded all the way over unbroken roads.

The final selection shows how MacEwan's interest in a farming career was re-directed by his father into enrollment in the Ontario Agricultural College in Guelph. Had not Grant obeyed his father's wishes, he might never have left the farm.

May, 1921 For some time I have been aspiring to start farming for myself. I have considered buying a Hudson Bay quarter, homesteading at Pleasantdale and purchasing a quarter from my father. I approached my sire with a proposition whereby I was to buy the northwest quarter from him and pressed my case enthusiastically. It was all without avail and the net result of my failure to get started caused me to consider going to an agricultural college.

Bertha Grant MacEwan (mother) and Grant, c. 1919

I considered Saskatchewan's Agricultural College and Ontario Agricultural College. The latter had this advantage that should I decide to attempt to switch from associate to degree, I could do it more easily and also save one year. *September 12, 1921* Decided to go to O.A.C., Guelph to take associate course in agriculture. I didn't have much money and therefore endeavored to find a cheap way of getting down. Malcolm McPhail was going to ship a car of cattle to Toronto and I got permission to travel with them. *September 15, 1921* Left Melfort with McPhail's car of cattle billed for Toronto. It was my first real break from the family ties and the departure was hard. The entire experience—brand new. My entire wardrobe and belongings were packed in one old telescope valise and the outfit hardly became a young man starting off for college. My clothing consisted of one old suit (the one I was wearing), one shirt in addition to the one on my back, one extra pair of sox, no nightgown or pyjamas, and one pair of cheap dress boots which gave me pain every time I moved. *September 22, 1921* Arrived in Toronto. Visited Eatons and bought a suit which never fitted me and a hat ten years out of date.

Went up to Guelph by Radial and proceeded to 228 Glasgow Street where I found Grandfather MacEwan alone in the house. He gave me a most hilarious welcome. Annie and Willa and Jim arrived home later in the evening. **Editor's Note:** Grandfather MacEwan was Alexander MacEwan's father. The house was kept by daughter Annie, who besides looking after her father, also tended her invalid brother Jim. Willa was a niece orphaned at a young age.

◆◆◆◆◆

II
The College Years
1921-1928

Grant MacEwan had just turned 19 when he began his freshman year at Guelph in September, 1921. Unlike many people, he does not refer to his childhood as carefree or fun-filled. Childhood, like adulthood, meant duties, tasks and accomplishments within a strong and supportive family unit. In this respect, MacEwan's transition from boy to man was marked by no significant change in behaviour or attitude.

During the period 1921-1928, Grant MacEwan received his professional training, graduating with a B.S.A. from the Ontario Agricultural College (O.A.C.) in Guelph in 1926. Two years later he received his M.S. from Iowa State College. Following this he accepted a position as Assistant Professor, Animal Husbandry, University of Saskatchewan, offered by W.J. Rutherford. He began his duties in July, 1928.

MacEwan spent five years at Ontario Agricultural College, Guelph. During the first two years he took an associate course in agriculture with certification upon successful completion. This provided a chance to move into a full degree programme. Designed for rural students who, for practical reasons had been unable to complete normal high school requirements, this option appealed to MacEwan.

As a student he was both conscientious and able. One excellent account covers his participation on the prestigious O.A.C. livestock judging team. His summer jobs and several business ventures further contributed to a growing sense of financial independence.

Grant MacEwan also entered fully into the spirit of college life, becoming involved in the usual array of zestful campus activities. He also emerged as a fine athlete. Though prominent in track and field, he was probably most proficient on the basketball court where he was a member of Ontario Agricultural College's winning intercollegiate team in 1925.

Following graduation in 1926, MacEwan returned to Melfort. He remained

Ontario Ag. College Basketball Team, Intermediate Intercollegiate Basketball
Champions, Guelph. Grant second from left, 1925

in the west until fall, 1927, when he returned to university. During these 16 months,
MacEwan tried drama and political campaigning, helped tend the family farm,
and worked in the livestock branch of the Saskatchewan government.

The period 1926-27 clearly marked a crossroads in MacEwan's life. He had
no desire to remain with the livestock branch with its excess of office work.
However, when other job opportunities in Ontario and Alberta failed to materialize,
he began to consider graduate work in agriculture. His subsequent application
to Iowa State College was unexpectedly rewarded with a Meat Fellowship. He
left for Ames, Iowa, in September, 1927.

MacEwan enjoyed both graduate school and the United States. His diary entries show him as less boisterous and more mature than when at Guelph. For
example, his reference to church-related activities is more pronounced here than
anywhere else in the journals. His professional capabilities were also coming to
the fore. When he graduated with his M.S. in May, 1928, he had several career
options. One was to continue research at the University of Chicago, but the Saskatchewan Agricultural Department also made him a firm offer. The most appeal-

ing, however, was the potential assistant professorship in animal husbandry at the University of Saskatchewan. At $2,500 a year, the opportunity to both teach and do field work was impossible to ignore. So in July, 1928, a month before his twenty-sixth birthday, Grant MacEwan began the first of several professional careers.

This journal selection is interesting historically for two main reasons. As a firsthand account of student life in the early 1920's, it is not only illuminative for its own sake, but also suggestive of modern parallels. The role of accident and choice in life also comes through strongly in the MacEwan experience. While it is impossible to ignore the role of purpose and initiative in Grant MacEwan's life, the fact remains that he reacted swiftly and pragmatically to emergent situations. The road from Melfort to Guelph to Iowa to Saskatoon might well have forked in many places. Yet looking back over 60 years to what might have been, MacEwan offered this insightful commentary: "As a boy I held a kind of romantic dream of being in university work. It was always there in the back of my mind. Despite all of the things I had done up to that time, it remained as my purpose to be achieved if at all possible."

September, 1921   Enrolled at Ontario Agricultural College. Paid $63 fee. Took up residence at 32 Upper Hunt in old residence. Wilf Weber is my roommate. He is a degree man and I, *just* an associate.

October, 1921   Freshman initiation a brutal affair. We received the roughest initiation in the history of the college.

January 11, 1922   Reaves, Wilson, Dyer, Lawrence and I walked out to J.J. Elliot's farm to see the $30,000 Millhills Comet. It was a fourteen mile trip out and back and by the time we got back we were ravenously hungry. All we had on the tramp was one frozen turnip which agreed with me but gave the other boys a bad attack of diarrhea.

January 21, 1922   We had macaroni and hash for supper last night and with dire results. Activity began in the halls of the residence about 3:00 a.m. The bathroom equipment was only fifty percent adequate from that early hour on. Reaves said the noise of the toilet flush buttons in Upper Hunt sounded like a typewriter in action. Some of the boys took their text books to the bathroom, and those who got a late call failed to get accommodation here and went down to the gym. The Mac Hall girls not out for breakfast this morning.

Editor's Note: Mac Hall girls refers to the MacDonald Institute for Home Economics, also located on the Guelph campus. The girls shared the same dining room as the Ontario Agricultural College students.

January 23, 1922   Gave my first class speech. Topic—The International Livestock Show of 1921.

March 16, 1922   At annual indoor athletic meet. Was second in hitch and kick. I kicked 7'10'' while the winner kicked 8'2''.

   Appointed to initiation committee for next fall.

March 17, 1922   The members of our year paid tribute to St. Patrick by

Sunday afternoon football make-believe. Grant in middle with J.J. Brickley, his roommate, on his left.

donning green ties. The annual freshman-sophomore fight began at 9:30 and lasted for one hour. It began at the entrance to Dr. Hugo Reid's classroom and Doc, too, had a hand in the melee.

August 14, 1922 I drove D.N. Jamieson to Tisdale fair where he was scheduled to judge cattle, sheep and pigs. I did my first public judging on that occasion.

September 30, 1922 Registered at Ontario Agricultural College for my second year associate. Paid $63 fees. (Board and room $5.50 per week, tuition for non-residents of province $25 a term.) Living this year in 126 Maidens Lane with old Doc Paine from Orillia.

October 1, 1922 The annual flag fight between first and second years. We took the flag at eight minutes. Then followed the Initiation Memorial ceremony. Bill Reaves and I had a sad experience tonight. We are both from the prairies and both hungry for Ontario apples. Early in the day we spotted some good trees and tonight at a late hour we struck off to gather a supply of fruit. Bill had a pair of pyjamas with the leg bottoms tied and I took my pillow case. We got about all the apples we could carry and came back to residence to enter by the back way as quietly as possible. Our success in making our way unnoticed was A-1, until we reached the top of the stairway when my pillow-case, already groaning under the strain, broke and let my entire cargo rumble down the steps. I did not linger behind to pick up the fruit, but as speedily as possible made for cover while the dean of residence, and others not in bed at that late hour, came out to discover the cause of the noise.

October 16, 1922 Reaves and I went on another apple hunting expedition tonight. This time we made our way through a newly discovered hole in the orchard fence. Nothing more serious than Reaves falling out of a tree occurred. We got our apples home safely this time, but a bunch of cannibals in the residence got wind of our expedition and came around and ate most of them.

December 26, 1922 Fared very well. A parcel from home contained a cake, necktie, handkerchiefs, garters and armbands.

Barber phoned to say that Grandad will either have to pull down the blind or his shirt when he goes to bed. He cannot get his wife to go to bed.

January 24, 1923 Made class speech, "Women: Past, Present and Future."

March 17, 1923 The usual St. Patrick's fight between first and second years. The two years then combined against the fourth year and a notable and unprecedented water fight ensued. All I got out of it was a bruised hand, a cut head, a black eye and a general soaking.

April 10, 1923 Len Cavanah, I.S. McKay and I have organized a program of summer work. We will first of all proceed to McKay's town of Woodville and put in the crop there and plant some early spuds.

May 8, 1923 Cavanah, McKay and I bought a Model '18 Ford car for $175.00. Len says it goes downhill fine, but it ought to have a lantern hung on the front.

June 2, 1923 We went trout fishing in some of the beautiful streams of Durham county. We stayed all day and between the three of us, we got thirty-one speckled trout and had a whale of a day.

September 26, 1923 Arrived in Toronto at 7:00 a.m. I bought a grey suit at T. Eatons for $16.50. Also bought an overcoat. Travelled up to Guelph by radial.

September 27, 1923 Came to the college and donned my first rugby uniform.

September 28, 1923 Moved in. We dumped the freshmen tonight. Paid $65 in fees. I am going to room with J. Brickley, we will be in 300 Mills Hall.

Editor's Note: Joe Brickley came from a farm family in Napanee, Eastern Ontario, and had actually attended Ontario Agricultural College earlier. He and the tall, lean Presbyterian MacEwan made a strange pair. MacEwan recalls their first evening. Despite some misgivings, MacEwan got down on his knees at bedtime to pray. Half expecting taunts or mockery, he was somewhat surprised and relieved to find his new room-mate doing exactly the same thing. The two became firm friends.

Brickley left Ontario Agricultural College before graduation to take a position with the United Fruit Company in Cuba. MacEwan recalls that he was sorely tempted to go along. Brickley prospered in Cuba and later, British Honduras. At one time he was a good friend of Fidel and Raoul Castro. He retired to California and became wealthier through real estate dealings. For years MacEwan and Brickley retained an ongoing, though infrequent correspondence.

January 25, 1924 I have made a place on the Senior basketball team. Professor Baker is our coach, and although severe and hard-boiled, he can get results.

February 1, 1924 The conversat, which is the social event of the year, was staged tonight. It was a great success. My partner was Gladys Eaton. The third year is annually responsible for the conversat. That meant us, and we worked hard before and after the big event. Got to bed at 6:00 a.m.

February 27, 1924 Summer employment has not been decided upon yet. Not sure that I will go west or not, but did just today make application for a job as weed inspector in R.M. Star City.

March 26, 1924 Telegram. "George seriously sick. Dad."

March 27, 1924 Telegram. "George died last night." My reply: "Leaving tonight." I got the sad news at 3:00 p.m., and hastily consulted Professor Blackwood and the bursar. The former gave me sound advice and encouragement regarding the examinations now coming up. The boys (Brick especially) gave me a lot of help to get packed up. Aunt Annie and Aunt Aggie came up to see me, and I got away at 7:45 p.m.

April 1, 1924 Arrived home this morning. Jim Kilpatrick met me at the train at 5:00 a.m. Georgie's funeral was held this afternoon. Mother and Dad are completely broken, their very life seems snatched from them.

There was a beautiful service at St. James Church. The flowers were numerous. The hymns sung were "Rock of Ages," "Jesus Lover of My Soul," "My Times are in Thy Hands." Reverend Brydon conducted.

George had written his first spring examination a week ago Friday (March 21). He had a headache on Saturday, was quite sick on Sunday, unconscious on Monday and died Wednesday night from spinal meningitis. Mother and Dad were with him for the last day and a half, but he only once regained consciousness while they were there. That time he asked for a drink of water from the "tank." All the possible medical attention was given but without avail.

Editor's Note: The shock of losing brother and son was traumatic for the MacEwan family. George was to carry on the family farm, and was quieter and less gregarious than his older brother. According to MacEwan, George was extremely close to his parents.

April 8, 1924 Saddled a horse and rode to Star City to an R.M. council meeting. The roads are breaking up badly and progress was very slow and painful after the first few miles in the saddle. Twenty-four miles of these roads are far too many for a person riding for the first time in a year.

I signed a contract for the weed inspector work for R.M., Star City.

Editor's Note: Most of MacEwan's energies in weed extermination were directed against the sow thistle. "We did not exterminate the sow thistle but we gave them a bad scare and set them back a few years."

July, 1924 Melfort Summer Fair. I took two days off from weed work to show twelve head of our Angus cattle and four horses. The competition was keen but we fared very well and made $150 gross.

September 1, 1924 My season's work as a weed inspector was concluded today with a trip to Star City for the purpose of making final reports. I have collected $370 (74 days at $5 a day) which will pretty well take care of me for another year at college.

From the first of June until the present, I have driven the Carbert mare and our old buggy ten to twenty-five miles a day. The buggy has been threatening to collapse for years and at present there are three sizes of wheels on it, but it has served me well. I carried my dinner with me and came home at nights. The Melfort Fair offered the only diversion of the summer and that was profitable to me.

We have used crude oil on the smaller patches of sow thistle. It was awkward and costly and we looked for a better method. Sodium arsenite seemed to offer some possibilities and I was able to secure some for experimentation. A site near Stoney Creek was selected and the chemical was applied. Proceeding in that direction for the purpose of making observations one morning following the application, I paused to speak to the negro employed by Henry Harms. "You've gone and killed all Sam Boyle's cows with that dope of yourne." My heart sank, but I hastened on to learn the truth and it was bad enough. There I learned that "one cow dead, calves sick, and baby's got the diarrhea."

The saving of money was always a major purpose in our home, and the summer in question when I was striving to meet my next winter expenses was no exception. Total expenditure for selfish or personal reasons would not have bought a cheap hat and the clothes worn were of the most modest type. One pair of shoes was worn until it could not be brought home. It was on a wet morning in August, I decided that I should walk down the right-of-way from Melfort to Naisberry. The rain made my dilapidated shoes still less adequate and eventually they were so far gone that I could walk in them no further. I sat down to hold a lone council of war. Behold, within a rod from where I sat, I spied a pair of shoes which had been discarded, and which, upon inspection, proved vastly better than my own. I made a hasty change and strange to say, the new pair fitted me all right. Providence seemed to smile upon me on that occasion.

September 19, 1924   Arrived Toronto. Went on up to Guelph and paid college fees amounting to $73.75. That was a tough blow.

I will again room with Brickley. We went downtown today and bought two grey suits. By taking two of one kind we got them at $10 each. Mine fits! *October 10, 1924*   There was a successful barn dance of the Animal Husbandry Club. I played the part of a Highland Lassie for part of the evening and that of a black bear for that balance.

November 22, 1924   Returned today from the Royal Winter Fair, Toronto. I spent the week with Tommy Amos and Bill Black and secured some valuable experience. Tom Amos is the recognized dean of cattle showmen. Our white bull, Manor Chief ninth, won the aged class over the Prince's bull, King of the Fairies. It was a matter of great rejoicing.

On my return from Toronto at an early morning hour, my old mate, Brickley, raised up in bed and told me he had applied for a job in Cuba with the United Fruit Co.

December 9, 1924   Negotiated a deal whereby I will sell Ontario Agricultural
College cushion covers this Christmas. I bought the limited supply of these
articles on sale in the city and figure I have a corner or monopoly on that
trade now. Should be able to make 75 cents each on them.

December 22, 1924   There was great excitement this forenoon when a cottage down College Avenue took fire. We were on the scene with the college
hose line before the city fire department got there, much to the disgust of
the city firemen. I got properly soaked when on the roof and then my clothes
froze. If that kind of treatment will give a man a cold, we'll know tomorrow.

January 7, 1925   Harry Miller and I were awarded the tender on the refresh-
ment booth at the rink. We plan on big business. The tender cost us $35.
Editor's Note: They sold hot dogs at the college rink and made a little money.
Harry Miller was a Nova Scotian, "an older old-fashioned fellow who wore well."

January 8, 1925   The rink opened and we are selling. Business good for
the start.

March 11, 1925   The Ontario Agricultural College first basketball team
played Osgoode Hall in the deciding game of the league. We won by 25 -
16 and are now intermediate intercollegiate champions. There were 500 spectators, 100 of which were drunk. The drunks were Osgoode's supporters.
They came by a special radial and arrived late. At Georgetown, six of them
stood on the sidewalk and wrote names in the snow. The police waited at
the depot for them while they all got off at Bay. Throughout the game some
of them fought, some sang and some slept. We are told that eleven were carried off at Toronto on their return.

April 16, 1925   I took the 7:30 train for Belmont, arrived there at 10:00
a.m., drove out to Basil Robinson's farm, had dinner, bought a bull, Questa
of Raydale for $160.00, brought him back to town and had him loaded and
shipped at 1:15 p.m. Fair good speed. I am travelling with the bull. We got
back to Brandon at 4:00 and we'll go to Melfort via Portage and Dauphin
and Humboldt.

April 20, 1925   Arrived home. Dad is very well pleased with the bull. He
is a trifle slack back of the shoulders and heart, but is a meaty creature with
great thighs and loin.

May 23, 1925   Bill Wood's house caught fire today and created a sensation.
The fire was in the attic and well started around the chimney. They called
for help and Jack Munroe and I ran to the scene. Arriving, we found the
people excited and helpless and all the water used up to no avail. I climbed
up the hatch in the ceiling, located the flames, and with the buttermilk and
cream which Jack located in the kitchen, the fire was extinguished.

September 15, 1925   Beginning today we pursue a position on the Ontario
Agricultural College Livestock judging team to Chicago in no uncertain way.
We will first of all take a ten-day tour of livestock establishments in eastern
Ontario.

Throughout my college career, my hopes have focused upon the Chicago judging team more than anything else and it was this and lower living expenses and tuition that motivated me to Ontario Agricultural College rather than some other institution. Today our senior class, every member of which is keen to make a place on the team, left Guelph in five autos to broaden our knowledge of types and to score among the top five if possible.

The first stop today was made at Joe Wilmot's where we judged Hampshire sheep. Then at General Greenlie's, we had a lunch at the old chap's hand and then worked over the Herefords on the farm. The herd bull is by Gay Lad Fortieth and is small but nice. The General is a single man and has no apology to make.

The next stop was at Battie Bros. for Percherons. We went in to Toronto and stopped at the Carls Ritz for the night.

We judged two classes of grand heavy geldings at the Toronto Transport Co. where 300 head of horses are kept. Next we judged two classes of heavy Express horses at the City Dairy, then three classes of same kind at Farmer's Dairy. Here, too, I was introduced to C. acidopholis milk. There are over 300 horses in barns of the City Dairy.

September 16, 1925 To the farm of Harry McGee, Islington, where we worked Shorthorns and Yorkshires. Then to Thomas Russel's Shorthorn farm at Downsview. At Clarkson's farm we judged two classes of Leicesters and then proceeded to Stoddard's for steers. The last place today was that of Stan Gaurdhouse where we judged steers. We had the grand champion steer at the recent C.N.E. in one class. Yesterday my judgment was rotten and I could see my chances for Chicago fading, but today has been not bad.

September 17, 1925 First stop this morning was Frank Batty's Whitby for Clydes. We had an excellent lot of mares to work with. While there we had a chance to inspect the Government owned stallion, ''Mainring,'' who was grand champion at Glasgow, Scotland, Toronto and Chicago in 1923. He is a good-boned horse with a deep but narrow body.

Bill Dryden's place at Brooklyn was visited. There we saw the imported ''Quarterstaff,'' and judged two classes of Shorthorns. From Dryden's we went to Robert Duff and Son farm at Ashburn for horses, then to John Miller's for Shropshires and lastly to Torrance's at Markham for Clyde stallions. Back to Toronto tonight. We gave reasons on a number of our classes this evening. Poor old Baldy had a hard time convincing Professors Toole and Steckley that his decision of Markham's stallions was right. Baldy questioned if one of them could hope for posterity.

September 18, 1925 Donalda Farms are a treat. We spent most of today on the estate. It is eight miles out of Toronto and is on the Don River. Some of the profits from the Hollinger gold mine went into this show place. The deceased owner of Donalda was one of the largest shareholders in the mine. The dairy stable alone cost $60,000 and it is kept spotless. We are told that the annual deficit on the farm runs around $50,000. Dr. Jenkins is at present in charge of the farm, and he certainly made things pleasant and interesting for us. We had an elegant dinner at the farm camp. I have never seen such butter-colored whipped cream as was lavishly served to us. We judged 15 classes of pure-bred stock consisting of Holsteins, Guernseys, Shorthorns, Jerseys, Leicesters, Yorkshires and Berkshires.

We made one brief call after Donalda and it was for Jerseys at R.J. Fleming's place. (He is President of Toronto Transport Co.)

September 19, 1925 At W.E. Watson's this morning (Woodbridge) for Draught horses and Holstein cattle. We had dinner in Brampton and saw the sign in the restaurant window "We Sell only Bull's Milk." After dinner we went to B.H. Bull & Sons' well-known establishment for Jerseys, and then headed for Guelph.

September 23, 1925 The race for a place on the judging team becomes warmer and keener as the days go by. Our coaches, Wade Toole, Jack Steckley, Bill Knox and George Raithby, are all very able and the chief, Wade Toole, is "one in a million."

Editor's Note: MacEwan speaks fondly about Wade Toole, Head of the Department of Animal Husbandry at Guelph. He was a big man, somewhat autocratic but a good teacher. He also had a sense of humour.

September 25, 1925 The selection of the judging team was partly completed today. Seven men (from which five men to judge and two spares will be named later) were selected today. I am rejoicing at being AMONG THE SEVEN.

November 11, 1925 Our judging team left Guelph for Toronto. Wade Toole announced four of the five men to judge in the Royal Competition tomorrow. They are Knox, Cruickshank, Simpson and myself. Then he flipped a coin to see if Herb Hannam or Archie McGuigan would be fifth man. The latter won.

November 12, 1925 Toronto Royal judging competition. Ontario Agricultural College wins, Manitoba second and Alberta third. I was high man on our team and high in the intercollegiate competition, although won no first in individual classes.

November 13, 1925 Dean Howes of the University of Alberta addressed the student body tonight. He said with the Greeks, agriculture was an occupation for men of noble birth. He also stated that he had taken a keen interest in athletics. "I do not curl, I have not fallen for that foot and mouth disease, golf, but find great delight in following the students in rugby, hockey and basketball."

November 20, 1925 Our judging team embarked for the States. The Ontario Government is assisting us financially for which we are truly grateful. We left at 5:40 p.m.

November 21, 1925 Arrived at Lansing, Michigan and stopped at the Roosevelt Hotel. We spent most of the day judging hogs, horses, sheep and beef cattle at M.A.C. We were fed and watered at noon, the guests of Fergy Ferguson (OAC'21). Left at 7:30 p.m. for Detroit and Lafayette, Indiana.

November 22, 1925   At Lafayette. Slept and went to church today. Poor old Wade Toole has a violent attack of diarrhea. Bill Knox said Wade took enough essence of wild strawberry to block a sewer.

November 28, 1925   This was the big day of our young lives. The competition made an extremely heavy day. We were under constant escort from 7:00 a.m. until 7:30 p.m. We judged 12 classes and gave oral reasons on eight of them. We were dog-tired tonight and went to our hotel after our release. Wade Toole brought the good news after midnight. McGuigan high man, Knox fourth, MacEwan sixth, Cruickshank forty-first and Simpson sixty-ninth. Ontario team third.

December 3, 1925   Arrived back at Guelph and were met by the student body. They had the band and three vehicles for our transportation. It was a grand reception and it continued into the evening in Mills Hall.

March 16, 1926   We had a very notable basketball game between the third and fourth years. The third year men were confident of success and so were we. I was detained at Barbers Slaughter House and an SOS call came for me. I ran and stole rides all the way home. A lot of money was up on both sides and the game was featured by enthusiasm, fights, etc. We won by a nice margin.

March, 1926   Jim Simpson and I are working together on our thesis on "Crossbreeding in the Production of Market Pigs." We have been conducting a feeding trial and carefully checking the carcasses, counting ribs (about the first systematic work done on rib variations in pigs), measuring intestines, etc.

May 28, 1926   Along with 33 of year 1926 men, I received my B.S.A. degree. For the first time the convocation exercises were held in Guelph, the University of Toronto Senate coming up.

May 31, 1926   I left dear old Guelph for Saskatchewan. I wonder if I'm right. Here in Ontario there is a job at Gunns Limited buying cattle, and later in the year there is district representative work for me, and out west there is just "home." I plan to return in the fall and accept the "rep." work promised me.

June 5, 1926   Arrived home at Melfort. The seeding is about completed. I have received a gold Waltham watch from Mother and Dad in recognition of the event of May 28.

June 18, 1926   I received a call from J.G. Robertson, Livestock Commissioner, Regina, to join the Cattle Improvement Train. I proceeded today and joined the train at Lockwood. I am to assist in a general way and do a little lecturing.

Editor's Note: The Cattle Improvement Train toured the province interacting with farmers through lectures, exhibitions and personal dialogue. It was designed to educate farmers by acquainting them with the latest developments in agriculture. J.G. Robertson was a distant relative of MacEwan's mother.

June, 1926   Professor Jackson of Manitoba Agricultural College (M.A.C.)

Grant with his first car, a Model T. Paid $150. c. 1923.

was a member of the staff of the lecture cars. He was talking forestry. We were camped for Sunday on the west side of Watson. Professor Jackson was very enthusiastic about the value of ultra-violet light, and each day he found a secluded spot where he could expose his carcass to the sun. At Watson the facilities were ideal. A small slough lay beside the railway track, and beyond the slough was a thick fringe of bushes. It offered a splendid opportunity for sun bathing when the fringe of protection on the west side and the train on the east side of the dry slough gave such good concealment. Sunday afternoon found Jackson parading in the nude on the train side of the bushes. Gus Couch, an untiring woman chaser, arranged to meet two girls at the train at 3:00. (Gus had a particular flair for the daughters of town mayors.) At 3:00, the girls drove up in their car and stopped between the train and the bushes. Jackson, to the amusement of the girls, lost no time in gaining the shelter of the bush. But Jackson, willing to amuse the girls some more, found an old apple barrel in the trees. He got into same and returned to the open to talk with the girls and cut some capers for their benefit. He clipped his heels together and made some quick moves, but had not reckoned with the durability of the barrel. One stave in the barrel gave way and as if shot from a gun, the entire barrel collapsed, leaving poor old Jackson standing before the car with no other protection than the hoop which he continued to hold. The 100 yards from that point to the back of the trees were made in ten flat.

July 24, 1926   I have received a letter from John Rayner of the Extension Department, University, Saskatoon asking me to judge cattle, sheep and swine at Canora, Kamsack, Togo, Vonda, Wapella, Broadview, Whitewood and Grenfell. I left Melfort for Canora today.

July 26, 27, 1926   Canora Summer Fair. This marks my debut as an official judge of livestock. Met Brother Boles. He smokes a wicked pipe when away from home. We had 60 head of cattle, 25 hogs and nine sheep in the competitions.

August 28, 1926 I have been recruited by O.D. Hill to do some work in the forthcoming federal campaign. Tonight I went with O.D. Hill to hold a meeting at Fairy Glen.

Editor's Note: O.D. Hill was a Melfort lawyer and the campaign manager of Malcolm McLean. This marked MacEwan's first formal political activity.

August 30, 1926 Went to North Star to assist with a meeting on O.D. Hill's behalf.

September 2, 1926 It has been raining for four days. St. Clair Hatton, Jim Gale and I pushed our ways through the mud and conducted a campaign meeting at Central Park.

September 9, 1926 Meeting at Clapton. H.A. MacEwan and I took it. There were only 20 out and half of them were Conservatives.

September 14, 1926 MacKenzie King returned to power in today's federal election. Malcolm McLean of Eldersley (local candidate) got a majority of about 3,000. I was agent for McLean at Pleasant Valley poll and Dad was returning officer. The Valley, for the first time in history, gave a Liberal majority of nine (53 - 62).

September 16, 1926 Having accepted an offer of further work with the Provincial Livestock Branch, I left Melfort this morning on the 5:30 train (fare to Regina $10.85).

September 17, 1926 Began work with the Branch. My first job was hanging pictures in the office at the Parliament Buildings.

September 18, 1926 I moved up to Jack Munroe's home this evening and will try boarding there.

September 20, 1926 Had supper with O.D. Hill, George Mantle (Clerk of Legislature), Sam Latta (Minister of Education) and Mr. Perrin Taylor (Deputy Provincial Treasurer).

September 21, 1926 Faring very well. Tonight I dined with Malcolm McLean, M.P. and D.A. Hall, M.L.A. for Cumberland. Hall lives at Lac Laronge and prefers it to Regina. I have an invitation to visit him.

September 23, 1926 I saw two coyotes in front of the Parliament Buildings this morning.

October 7, 1926 I made application today for the position of assistant to superintendent at the experimental station at Lacombe, Alberta.

Coaching junior rugby team but it is a discouraging business. Rugby players in this city appear to believe that to play that game, one must drink and smoke and fight and swear and practise Sunday morning, etc.

November 1, 1926 Got my October pay cheque—$137.50.

November 2, 1926 I attended the Regina sheep and swine show today. Professor Wade Toole is judging hogs. Good to see the old giant. This evening there was the customary tug-of-war between the sheep men and hog men.

I pulled with the winners—the hog men.

December 25, 1926 At home all day. I have persuaded Mother and Dad to take a holiday at the West Coast and I will remain home and hold the fort.

January 3, 1927 I had a phone message from J.G. Robertson, livestock commissioner, asking if I would return at once and conduct some work for the branch at Moose Jaw. My reply was "No." I will run the farm this winter.

January 5, 1927 I'm alone on the farm and have about 60 head of cattle, horses and a house full of hens. Mother left bushels of food including two large batches of brown bread (the kind of black stuff which she alone can make) and froze it in the fresh state. I've also laid in a pail of jam and a case of canned tomatoes.

January 17, 1927 Batching is going fine. Meals served at all hours. I baked a pan of biscuits and the dog liked them so well that I gave him the entire batch. D.N. Jamieson has been here twice for meals. I told him that if he took a good dose of salts prior to one of my meals and another after, the chances are that the meal would never hurt him.

About 40 degrees below this morning and much of the day. One old hen laid a frozen egg. Some of the neighbours thought that a joke but the poor old hen didn't see the joke.

January 24, 1927 Forty-four below this morning. When I was through milking, I had a pail full of shreds which looked like macaroni. Each squirt of milk froze before it settled.

February 13, 1927 We are preparing for a play at Pleasant Valley. It necessitates two to three night practices a week and the sensation of arriving home to a cold house at or after midnight is not to be envied.

February 16, 1927 Beauty calved rather unexpectedly this afternoon. I put the cattle out this morning and went to the valley this afternoon, returning about 3:30. Immediately upon my return I put the cattle in the stable but old Beau was missing. My next job was to find Beauty and her calf. I was sure the latter, if born on this severely cold day, would be dead, but I was hopeful. I hitched the big team to the stoneboat and began the search. It was bitter cold and darkness was falling. After exploring the bluffs, I turned to a straw pile on the southeast quarter and, sure enough, there was Beauty and her bull calf—the calf quite white with frost. It was badly frozen but still alive. I placed it on the boat and held it there while I drove with one hand. It was cold. I froze several fingers before I got home but that was all right as long as I saved that bull calf.

February 17, 1927 Beauty's calf is living in the kitchen of the house along with me. I brought him in to get thawed out last night and each time I return him to the barn he freezes again. His tail and ears become quite stiff and even his nose freezes. It looks as if I'll have to keep him in the house all winter even though his house manners are the worst in the world. I carry him to the stable for a suck about five times during the day, and he is awfully happy to suck in the stable and sleep in the house.

February 18, 1927 We staged our play "In Hot Tamale Land" at Pleasant Valley Community Hall. It was a good success and the hall was filled.

February 20, 1927 Beauty's calf is still in the house and his manners are not improved. I plan to try him in the stable again tomorrow and to protect his ears I have made him a cap or head gear out of an old sweater. It has the dandiest ear pockets. I will also bandage his tail and put him right in an old woolen sweater.

February 22, 1927 We staged our play at Pathlow before a house crowded to capacity. One hundred and ninety paid admissions and some were turned away.

February 24, 1927 At the request of a Melfort organization, we staged our play in the Melfort theatre before 300 people. Had supper at the Ozark after the performance.

March 1, 1927 Attended a public lecture in Melfort by J.G. Haney of the I.H.C. demonstration farms. Then I stayed up all night to write the lecture up for *Melfort Moon*.

Editor's Note: J.G. Haney was a representative of International Harvester. MacEwan's report on the lecture for the *Melfort Moon* marked his first piece of public writing.

March 11, 1927 Poor old faithful Scotty was sick last night and I thought he was going to pass out but he is somewhat brighter looking today. I was moved to writing a poem to him last night, but my poetry is so rotten that when I wrote a poem to a dying dog, the dog didn't die.

To Scotty

Scotty old boy, you're going
Tomorrow will see the end
And none other will heed the difference
But I who'll have lost a friend.

You are only a canine brute lad,
You are only a dog, that's true,
But I know you would do for me lad
All that any human would do.

Oh Scotty my pal, I'll miss you,
You so willingly played your part,
But I'll miss you most old fellow,
For the trueness of your heart.

Would to God there were men like dogs
With hearts as true as steel
No jealousy, hatred, malice or pride,
And never a rotten deal.

You've done your duty well, boy,
You've done all that dog could do
And when I'm going lad, I hope
I have as few regrets as you.

So good-by Scotty, old Pal
The best of friends must part
This cold world will be colder
Without your soft warm heart.

For a dog, though true and trusty
No Heaven is in store
Should not we with a higher faith and hope
Be worthy of the other shore.

You were not much to look at lad,
You had no pedigree
You would not bring a dollar bill
But you just suited me.

It isn't "the looks" that make the pal
Nor pedigree that makes the friend
And money's worth is not here or there
But friendship makes the friend.

Paul Bunyan

April 21, 1927 Shipped six fat calves. I took them in two loads of three calves each and had a tough time. The roads are wretched. I upset once with three cattle and if it was not for Walter Grainger's help, I would never have got my loads all the way to town. (Wpg. price was $8.75 per cwt.)

May 31, 1927 Finished seeding wheat, 265 acres.

June 1, 1927 Left the farm at Melfort in Dad's care and went to Regina to work again with the Livestock Branch. I took a room with Dave Owens at 2151 Broad.

June, 1927 I am preparing to move to the country around Govan and Nokomis to do survey and field work for the Pure Bred Sire Areas Scheme. The Pure Bred Sire Areas Act came in this past winter and the hope is that scrub sires, particularly bulls, will be driven out.

June 17, 1927 Mr. Jas. Browne joined me in the work today. He is a great old character, sixty-two years old, short, a bachelor and minus a hand. He is a great student, although impractical in many respects.

Editor's Note: MacEwan was intrigued by James Browne, his partner on the Pure Bred Sires inspection work. A homespun philosopher with a wealth of personal anecdotes, Browne was a one-armed, crusty old Scot and a one-time President of the Saskatchewan Livestock Breeders' Association.

June 18, 1927 Mr. Browne left for home this morning.

June 20, 1927 Mr. Browne returned tonight and has not been in bed since the night before his departure from Nokomis. He spent last night in his car in a slough and read all night.

Mr. Browne is the youngest of the family of eight, is over fifty now and not one of them has married. He approves of marriage but objects to all the darned preliminaries. If the government had allotted him a woman, he would have taken her for better or for worse, but he would never court one.

He was telling me today that in Scott's day in Scotland, cattle were only counters—mine today and yours tomorrow.

June 22, 1927 A man by the name of Sid Love farms west of Nokomis. It is his boast that he gets the exact percentage of fillies and horse colts desired. To get a mare colt, he faces the dam north when breeding. The man has four boys and four girls. After each respective child was born, the bed was changed to face the opposite direction. This is just one more theory.

Mr. Browne thinks we should carry a can of red paint and systematically place a daub on every gate through which we drive and on every farmer to which we talk, so there would be less confusion and duplication.

Jas. Browne, "You can't stunt babies and raise men and you can't stunt calves and raise cattle. And to avoid the condition of stunting, attention is necessary. Very few farmers have time to give their calves the attention they require and very few know how. The farmer should be an efficiency man and have laborers to do the work. Fewer farms and more workmen is the solution. Three percent of our farmers are fit to farm and the rest should work for them."

June 30, 1927 I asked Mr. Browne if he had ever played rugby. "Goodness yes, Heaven for me will be one continual game of rugby. I'll be 'half' on one side and Michael, the arch-angel on the other." I said to Mr. Browne, "You should try to be on the same side as Michael." He—"No, no, I want a good man against me. No good playing against a second-rate man."

My old pal, Jimmy, says if people would eat less and run more, there wouldn't be so much sickness.

Mr. Browne and I were looking over a bunch of cattle. I said there were two scrub bulls. He said there were three. In the course of our disagreement, I stated that he had seen one bull twice; that a scrub bull was so quick and wiry that he could easily worm through the herd and appear in another place and the onlooker might not realize that he has seen the same bull twice. He (strong for annihilation of scrub bulls)—"All right, perhaps you're right, but I'll insist that we castrate him twice and be sure of him."

August 20, 1927 Ed Ridley bought my Ford coupe after much deliberation. I am going home to Melfort and then to Ames, Iowa for graduate studies. I have been offered a fellowship at Ames worth $540.00 and I've written to accept it. It is a fellowship in "meats."

September 16, 1927 Once more I leave old Melfort and all the friends there.

Today I am on my way to Winnipeg and from there I go to Ames, Iowa.
September 22, 1927 I was due at Ames at 9:00 last evening, but didn't
get there until this morning. It was this way. Leaving home I had a ticket
as long as my leg and each conductor seemed to delight in taking a piece
or pieces off it. Eventually I gave the last piece to the conductor on the last
division out of Ames and he, as usual, gave me a receipt. The car was hot
and I was tired and I went to sleep just out of Ames a piece. The trainman
came in and gathered the checks and announced "Ames next." I slept on.
At a later hour in the evening, I was awakened by the conductor who said
"ticket please." I awakened with a start and looked for my ticket, then
remembered that I had given it to him. "I gave it to you, there's my receipt—
no darn it, it's gone too." The conductor asked, "Where are you going?"
I replied, "to Ames" and it was then that I heard, "Hell, we've left Ames
an hour ago." He was mad and I was just as mad, but he finally offered
a way out. He suggested that I go to sleep again and go to Des Moines (just
another few minutes run) and he would take me back to Ames on the next
train, about three hours hence. I didn't get much real sleep last night.

I went up to the college today, met my future chiefs, Professors Helser
and Kildee. They both look fine to me. Also found old Doc Staples of Guelph
'24 and it looks as though I'll have to live with old Doc. I took up residence
(room only) at Mrs. Cramer's, 2519 Hunt Street. Registered at the college.
Taking eight hours Meats; two hours Experimental Methods from J.M. Ev-
vard and five hours Comparative Physiology from Dr. Bergman. Also visiting
a class in Biometrics and one in Breeding.
October 3, 1927 I went to church twice today. Tonight I was at the Methodist
Church and heard the Krantz Family Orchestra. It was very good but anything
Yankee Doodle is called sacred here.
October 17, 1927 Doc Staples and I were guests at supper at Alpha Gamma
Rho House. There's a fine bunch of fellows. They are courtesy and
friendliness itself.
October 23, 1927 Heard a real unadulterated gospel sermon at Chapel,
delivered by Archbishop, J.J. Keane of the Catholic Church. His theology
and mine, in spite of outward differences, appear to harmonize as far as fun-
damentals are concerned.
October 30, 1927 Heard Maxwell Nicy Hayson, a Negro poet and musician, at the Presbyterian Church. He read and played on his own composi-
tion and also recited some of Paul Dunbar's (negro poet) pieces.
November 24, 1927 Thanksgiving Day. I attended a morning service at
which President Hughes spoke. In enumerating his blessings he said, "First
of all I am thankful for faith in a personal God and for the power of prayer.
That may seem unscientific but it's like listening to a radio which is giving
music from Australia. I can't believe it possible, *but it works.*"
December 10, 1927 Professor Helser left for his home, having received
word of his father's serious illness. I am left with my work, his classes, and

a lot of experimental work we were doing together.

Am informed that no less than three graduate students have gone.

January 19, 1928 Addressed the Cosmopolitan Club on "Canada."

Took in the graduate club dance. My partner was Harriet Brigham. After the dance I went to work and set up my rat feeding project. I did not go to bed at all this night, but worked right through until class time in the morning.

January 24, 1928 Spoke at Lion's Club luncheon downtown today. I had a double topic as requested—Canada and Robert Burns. The club members are a nice lot, mostly businessmen and some faculty members.

February 29, 1928 While acting boyish in the meat lab, I connected with a concrete girder and opened my scalp. Six stitches were required, and the old army doctor who did the sewing would not have been any rougher if he had been sewing an old potato bag. Worst of all, I'm missing a leap year dance by virtue of my wound and clipped hair. I had accepted the invitation and was advised by the little lady that she would call with a taxi at 8:00 p.m.

March 8, 1928 I attended the Phi Kappa Phi initiation banquet. It was rare. The subject of the toasts was "Creative Genius."

April 7, 1928 Accompanied Edna Rhodes to a "fire-side" at Professor Mervine's home. Professor Mervine's testimony was good. He said that in his younger days, with a scientific outlook he tried to obtain material proof for what he believed. He tried to believe that Jesus knew some special medicinal properties in the clay which he used to open the eyes of the blind, but now he doesn't look for proof. The miracles recorded, he says, are without a doubt facts, and the many young minds who today are endeavoring to evade belief in the Bible, will outgrow their scepticism. He testified to faith in Jesus and prayer.

April 20, 1928 I have been in possession of a letter from Mr. Auld of Regina offering me a position with the Livestock Branch. I had hoped something else would open up but I can't afford to take a chance of being out of a position, and I have today decided to accept Mr. Auld's offer.

May 11, 1928 Final oral examination. My examining committee consisted of Professor Helser (Chairman), Professor Culbertson, Professor Shearer, Dr. Bergman and Dr. Mable Miller. Many and varied were the questions and concerned feeding babies, selecting cattle with bigger livers, Eskimos, etc. It all lasted one and three-quarter hours.

May, 1928 A wire from Dean Rutherford of University of Saskatchewan, Saskatoon, read "Are you in position to consider offer of Assistant Professor of Animal Husbandry at University of Saskatchewan. Wire collect."

I had written to Mr. Auld last night and finally accepted a position with him but I so much prefer to try university work that I have tonight written Mr. Auld asking that my letter of last night be ignored and that I be given some additional few days in which to make my final decision. My wire to Dean Rutherford could not indicate my entire joy and enthusiasm at the prospect of this new work. My prayers have evidently not been in vain.

Editor's Note: MacEwan was in the lab working when the wire from Rutherford came through. He took the call in the caretaker's office. He took the message down on a piece of scrap paper. Musing soon after on the contents of the wire, he turned the piece of paper over to find Tennyson's memorable line—"More things are wrought by prayer . . . " Even today, MacEwan remains convinced of the mystical coalescence.

May 31, 1928   A letter from Dean Rutherford in which he formally offered the position on the Animal Husbandry staff at University of Saskatchewan. I lost no time in forwarding my acceptance. I feel very happy about it.

June 11, 1928   Convocation. I received my M.S. degree.

June 12, 1928   I left dear old Ames and a lot of fine Iowa friends this morning at 7:00. It was pouring rain and I was soaked to the hide. The Iowa people are hard to leave. Now that my stay with them is past, I concluded that they are the friendliest and most courteous that I have ever mingled with.

June 15, 1928   Arrived once more at home at Melfort.

June 26 and 27, 1928   Along with Dad and D.N. Jamieson, spent a brief period of exploration and holiday at and around Nipawin. The Nipawin ferry was out on account of heavy floods and we were only able to get across the river in the basket on the ferry cable. "D.N." became seasick when half way across.

July 2, 1928   Today I travelled to Saskatoon where I hope to continue to work with the University of Saskatchewan.

July 3, 1928   Visited the University and became acquainted with my future colleagues. Had a chat with Dean Rutherford and went with Professor A. Malcolm Shaw to his home for dinner.

III
The Agriculturalist
1928-1936

Grant MacEwan spent eighteen years at the University of Saskatchewan before leaving in September, 1946, to assume the Deanship of Agriculture at the University of Manitoba. In many ways, the Saskatchewan years proved to be the most formative period in MacEwan's life, and for that reason are dealt with in two sections. The first covers the period 1928-36, where the reader is exposed to the development of MacEwan the Agriculturist. It is often forgotten in the wake of his later historical writings, political and public service activities, that Grant MacEwan was, for many years, a professional agriculturist with a national reputation.

MacEwan's fascination with the outdoors and the simple life comes through strongly in the boating expeditions with his friend and colleague, Al Ewen. The journal entries from these trips are reproduced unedited and in their entirety. The beginnings of his publishing career began during this period with several agricultural articles and the textbook, *The Science and Practice of Canadian Animal Husbandry*, co-authored with Al Ewen and published by Thomas Nelson and Sons in 1936. His marriage in 1935 to Phyllis Cline, a schoolteacher from Churchbridge, Saskatchewan, marked another important milestone, as did his trip to Great Britain in 1932 with a shipment of university experimental cattle. MacEwan later noted that the return trip via the new Hudsons Bay route marked one of the highlights of his life. He was the first passenger to clear customs at the new port of Churchill.

Other more developmental characteristics come through strongly in this section. MacEwan's nascent interest in history and his longstanding fascination with colourful individuals are clearly manifest. One can also discern an element of his disillusion with organized religion as a personal solace and guiding force. MacEwan's robust sense of humour, probably his most recognizable trademark, is more in evidence in those selections.

Finally, the reader is exposed to MacEwan's widening public horizons. He
did not confine himself to the University campus, but moved freely into the farms
and towns of Saskatchewan where he lectured, judged livestock, gave meat-cutting
demonstrations and advice. As a public speaker, he became increasingly in demand. By the end of 1936, the sum total of MacEwan's energetic commitment
to agriculture and, to a lesser degree, public service, had made him one of the
rural west's most identifiable figures.

September 3, 1928 Humans are funny. Sometimes I think I like them. At
any rate, there are no two alike. Today I took compassion on the old woman
whom I have frequently seen on the main street, always ill-clothed and the
very picture of poverty. Today her feet were well out and I think she could
have pulled her shoes up to her knees without trouble. Though she had her
shoes on, she was walking in her bare feet. Anyway, I stopped her and told
her that if she would come with me, I would get her a pair of new shoes.
At first she was skeptical, but at last we crossed the street in the direction
of Hudson Bay Co. Store. I proceeded first through the revolving door and
when I was part way through, she began to come through on the other side
of the axis. I was trapped and she continued to shove against the door which
refused to go backwards. I signalled through the glass and finally won that
round.

I asked a clerk to fit this lady with a pair of useful shoes. She insisted
that the shoes must be high–the higher the better. There were no high ladies'
boots in the store and I, at length, hinted to the clerk that she might try a
pair of boy's boots on the old girl. We did attempt to make a pair of boy's
boots attractive to her, but she soon scented an irregularity and in a haughty
manner she got up and left us. By this time we had some spectators and
I was left to enjoy the embarrassment alone. I could imagine the questions
the spectators were asking themselves, "Is she his wife?" "Is she his
mother?" etc. After I explained my appreciation to the clerk, I too slunk
away. Moral—"Have as little as possible to do with women."

September 6, 7, 1928 Maple Creek Fair. I judged all the livestock, cattle,
horses, sheep and pigs. I like this ranch atmosphere, and the people are as
natural as can be. I went to the dance put on tonight (September 7) and enjoyed it a lot. It was a real cowboy pow-wow.

November 16, 1928 1,060 head of calves are in Saskatoon today for distribu-
tion to boys and girls in the territory around Saskatoon. Sid Johns of the
Exhibition Board and the Saskatoon Board of Trade are taking responsibility
of the scheme. I helped today to do the sorting at the stock yards. The plan
is to bring all these calves back to Saskatoon next spring—have a fat calf
show, and then sell them all by public auction.

I have been working with E.E. Brocklebank in coaching the provincial
swim club winning team which will now represent Saskatchewan at the
Toronto Royal. The team is comprised of two Prince Albert girls.

November 20, 1928 Word has come through that the two girls forming the Saskatchewan Swim Club team at Toronto, have won the Robb trophy, symbolic of the highest win.

January 12, 1929 Guernsey Cattle Improvement Ass'n., at Guernsey. I talked on "Dairy Cattle Feeding Problems."

January 26, 1929 The Provincial Legislature Members visited Saskatoon. We staged a livestock and meats display for their benefit.

January 29, 1929 Three boys from 1st. year Associate class went to the Provincial Dairy convention at Prince Albert to enter the Judging competitions. I gave the boys some special coaching which appeared to be rewarded. One of our boys was the individual winner in the competitons.

June 1, 1929 My article "Some Pig Breeding Observations" was published in *Scientific Agriculture* for May.

July 4, 5, 6, 1929 Rosetown Fair. An excellent horse show and good cattle show. I was standing in front of the circular, high-walled speed drome in which the monkeys drive small cars at high rates of speed, one car went wrong and soared upward to come over the wall and light in a heap out in the midway. The monkey, scenting trouble, got clear of the car before it left the wall but thinking he should be hurt, he howled tremendously and struck off down the midway, howling as he went.

July 6, 1929 The fair was over tonight. I got a chance ride back to Saskatoon with Bill Mathers. It began to rain heavily and the roads were almost too much for us. Bill, at best, is the world's worst driver, but I took the wheel most of the way back to Saskatoon. We saw seven cars on their backs or sides in the ditch on the way in. Some day that road will have gravel.

August 12, 13, 14, 1929 Gravelbourg Summer Fair. This was a rare exhibition. The delegation which met us (Mr. Hartnett and I) at the station on our arrival, was most hospitable. One of the members made a speech and hoped we would enjoy our stay at that time. "Now," he said, "I want you men to go where you like and come when you like. We give you the key to our city." Whereupon he presented me with a bottle opener of the common type.

The last night of the show was given over to a big dance in the hall at the exhibition grounds. I arranged to go with Miss Margaret Des Marteau who was assistant secretary at the fair. I was to meet her at 9 P.M. at the entrance to the hall. Nine came and Margaret did not show up, then 10, and 11 and the same result. At 11:30 Margaret's sister came into the hall and I enquired to learn that Margaret was now outside the hall in a car. I said I would go out. To my surprise, I found the secretary of the fair and Margaret in the front seat of a car, both quite intoxicated. They were like all good French, still courteous. Margaret was apologetic and began to cry. I stayed with them to reason and before I left, they drove (five of us with Margaret's sister and friend) out a country road to have another drink.

Editor's Note: Maurice Hartnett was from Purdue, Saskatchewan. His wide background of experience in agriculture included agricultural editor of the *Western*

Producer; Deputy Minister of Agriculture for Saskatchewan and Extension Department representative for the University of Saskatchewan. It was in this latter capacity that he was judging with MacEwan. The latter judged horses and Hartnett judged cattle.

November 23, 1929 I addressed the annual meeting of the Saskatoon Herd Improvement Ass'n., and was named their honorary president for the coming year.

January 22, 1930 To Edmonton with the University of Saskatchewan hockey team. On our way to Edmonton, the boys over whom I was keeping casual vigil, were feeling hilarious. At North Battleford they left the train and decorated the station and our car with toilet paper. I was reading in the car and quite unconscious to their mischief. In came a huge town policeman and enquired who was responsible for these university boys. I confessed. Well, they were getting into trouble and would have to be reported. Who would they report this too? When the question was put to me, I hesitated and then said that if he insisted on reporting this episode to the University, he should write to J.W.G. MacEwan, University of Saskatchewan. That was all he required. He didn't take my name. When I arrived home from Edmonton, a letter reporting the event was waiting for me. I acknowledged the letter, stated my deepest sorrow that such a thing should have occurred and that was the end of the business.

April, 1930 I have been playing basketball with the Saskatoon Grads. We fought our way to the Provincial Finals, lost to the Regina Balmorals by 25 points on their floor in the first of the finals between north and south, then beat them by 29 points on our own floor, to win the provincial championship. On April 14 and 15 we met New Westminster Adanacs, last year's Dominion Champions and this year's winners of Alberta and British Columbia for the Dominion semi-finals. We lost both games and the Adanacs proceeded east to meet Winnipeg Toilers.

May 17-24, 1930 Prof. Shaw, Geo. Valentine of Matador Ranch, and I, travelled through southwest Saskatchewan and southern Alberta in search of heifers for the proposed breeding project at the Matador Ranch. The proposal is to place 4 herds of cows, namely Hereford, Shorthorn, Angus and Galloway on the ranch and put bulls of one breed to them each year. Three groups of cross-bred calves and one group of pure calves would be raised each year. The calves would come to the University for feeding at weaning time each year.

Editor's Note: The cattle breeding experiment was considered in a most progressive light and made a strong case for the principles of cross-breeding. Grant's later trip to England (1932) was with cattle bred from this programme. The detailed results of the programme were published by Shaw and MacEwan in *Scientific Agriculture*, the official publication of the Canadian Society of Technical Agricultures.

I may remember it as one of the embarrassing moments of my life. It occurred as Prof. Shaw and I drove into the town of Tompkins today. The changes of water had produced increased peristalsis in my intestinal region and the urge was so great that I suggested to Shaw that I would drop off and enter a conspicuous privately owned toilet while he drove on to the telephone office to make a long distance call. I entered this strange little out-house, locked the door and gained the relief I desired. But while I was there, the lady of the premises came from her residence and tried to gain entrance to the toilet. I sat quietly and when she called, "Who's there?", I was silent. She called again and still I chose to hide my identity. But her spite was great and she turned the trick upon me by bolting the door on the outside and walking away. I was left in a strange town, in a strange toilet and locked in. I began to realize the seriousness of my position and that Shaw would be waiting for me. I became rather desperate and, it was too bad, but the door had to be broken or I might have been there yet.

July 1, 1930   Donald McPhee and I judged in outside rings at Weyburn. There came a young man more concerned about the newness of his surroundings than where he put his feet. One freshly polished boot found its way into the heart of a fresh deposit of digested grass and with more of disgust than discretion, he gave a violent kick in the direction of friend Donald, leaving the latter with an artistic covering of green. That Scotch Presbyterian said a violent "damn."

July 14, 1930   With a University car I drove to a field day and farm tour programme at Silver Stream. We toured from farm to farm and discussed some phase of farm activity at each farm. An unusually fine farm garden was the center of attraction on one farm, Yorkshire hogs on another, Shorthorn cattle on another, artificial fertilizer plots on another and a farm dugout and reservoir on yet another.

Editor's Note: MacEwan, always very modest where his own achievements are concerned, has stated on occasion that he did help to bring the university to the farm. He did this partly by responding favourably to the Department of Extension's requests for service. The previous entry provides an example of this co-operation.

July 16, 1930   Lumsden Fair. I really believe that Lumsden has the nicest spot for a fairgrounds of any place in Saskatchewan. There are a lot of good livestock around Lumsden too.

August, 1930   Along with Joe Brickley, Ab Colbert and Harry Houghton, I saw Waskesui National Park. At the park for the first time I was inspired to talk freely and explore as much as possible. We were walking through the park in company with Miss Ruth Brown of Saskatoon and as we approached a beautifully made log building of cabin dimensions I was unfortunately moved to remark, "That's my ideal. I would like to spend the rest of my days here in the north and live in a structure like that." I understood why there was consternation in the party when I walked to the other side of the building and saw written over the door, the words "Ladies Toilet."

September 16, 1930 Mr. A.H. Ewen of Aberdeen, Scotland, who has been appointed Ass't. Prof. of Animal Husbandry, arrived in the city tonight. I agreed to meet him at the King George Hotel at 7 P.M. I was there and twice asked the little Chinese to page Mr. Ewen. The calls failed to arouse a response from any corner. About 8:30 Dr. Murray came in and asked if I had found Ewen. I said, "No," but I thought a man sitting over there looked like a brand new Scotchman even though he had not blinked an eye each time the page boy called. I said I would go over and ask the chap who he was. It was Ewen. He is a big, burly Scot, one who would never win a beauty competition, but an interesting and capable looking type.

Editor's Note: Al Ewen went on to become MacEwan's closest personal friend. A graduate of the University of Edinburgh, Scotland, Ewen was an excellent teacher and able "animal" man specializing in heavy horses. Following service in W.W. II he returned to the University of Saskatchewan and succeeded MacEwan as Head of the Animal Husbandry Department when the latter became Dean of Agriculture at the University of Manitoba in 1946. Ewen later returned to his native Scotland to farm.

October 31, 1930 At the teachers' Halloween Dance, held at Victoria School, I went with Marg Guest, but met another lady who rather caught my undivided attention. She was Phyllis Cline, somewhat of a show-girl type and a singer, but otherwise a very good looking kind to know.

November 11, 1930 Talked "Winter Steer Feeding" over radio *C.K.C.K.* The set up was in Mr. Clinkskill's room in college building and while I was talking, Mr. Clinkskill went to sleep and began to snore very loudly. I laughed and forgot what I had been saying. He said it was the first time he ever broadcasted.

December 20, 1930 Yesterday I assisted Al Ewen to buy a pair of skates and today he tried his new outfit. It was his first attempt to skate. I held his arm and we made three or four rounds on the rink. Nothing was said until we came to a stop. I asked the big Scot what he thought about it now. I expected some thoughtful philosophic observation. His reply after an instant was "It's bloody slippery."

February 3, 4, 1931 Brock and I drove to Wisetown where we staged the first meat cutting demonstration to be held in rural Saskatchewan. On the first day we slaughtered a steer, a lamb and 4 pigs, and the second day we were given over to demonstrations on cutting and curing. We were greatly encouraged with the project. We were the guests of Ernie Ewing who farms south of Wisetown.

Editor's Note: Brock is E.E. Brocklebank of the Extension Department, University of Saskatchewan. The meat-cutting demonstrations were a great success and continued to be in high popular demand over the years. MacEwan recalls that their original intent was not so much to teach meat-cutting, but rather to acquaint farmers and ranchers with the physiology of cattle.

August 20, 1931 Al Ewen and I were at the office late tonight and decided that if we are going to take any holidays this year we must take them right away. We investigated the canoeing between Waskesui and Montreal Lakes but it is not feasible just now. We resolved at 11 P.M. tonight to purchase four telephone poles tomorrow and make a raft with which to float down the Saskatchewan River.

August 21, 1931 At one o'clock P.M. Al and I met at the river bank, he with two packing boxes and our provisions, and I with the telephone poles and the rope with which to lash them together. We rolled the logs down to the water, one by one and as each was pushed out into the stream it was lashed to its mates.

We left Saskatoon via Saskatchewan River on a home made craft. It consisted of 8 logs each one representing one half of a 24' used telephone pole and when lashed together, they made a raft 12 feet long and 7 feet wide. The logs were lashed together at the ends with half inch manilla rope. A packing box 3' × 3' × 4' secured at one end of the craft, served as a shelter and place of repose. It was open at the one end, so that when sleeping we had the box for the protection of our heads only.

The crew consisted of two: my partner, Al H. Ewen, a true son of old Scotia, and myself. A supply of food consisting of bread, butter, bologna and chocolate bars was taken along and this supply plus an occasional fish helped considerably.

The time of our departure was 3:30 P.M. Weather at best is a hazard in Saskatchewan, but, on a camping trip or trip of exploration, it is almost sure to be at its worst. We bucked a strong north east wind the first afternoon and at times it appeared only a matter of opinion whether the current or the wind was having the most marked effect upon the progress of the travellers. With evening there came the finest lull with an overcast sky. We slept by spasms while the craft sailed slowly on, only occasionally requiring to be pushed off a rock or the shore. About midnight a violent storm arose, replete with high wind and lightning. The boat rocked and tossed about like a wild broncho instead of the 1500 lb. river going vessel she really represented. The sailors were wrought with some little fear and decided between yawns to put ashore if that were possible. The shore was reached with some difficulty and with still more difficulty one side of the 1500 lb. craft was hoisted sufficiently high on the shore line to give the voyagers a fair assurance of security. The next couple of hours were nerve wrecking indeed, but two tired travellers finally dozed off to sleep again, amid rain, thunder and the lashing of wild waters.

At 3.30 A.M. all was calm again and we pushed off. At 4:30 we stranded on a sand bar and the longer of the two travellers was awakened by the Aberdonian to render assistance. Wading and pulling and pushing were necessary for 100 yards of shallow water and all was well again.

Breakfast at 7 A.M. (3 courses) bread, butter and bologna.

The Saskatchewan River is a mystery. There are but few places where

MacEwan on raft trip down Saskatchewan River with Alistair Ewen.

we could not easily bottom it with a seven foot pole. Much of the bottom is covered with a peculiar shifting sand which seems firm until one puts his weight on it when it begins to give and flow away from under. The current is fairly fast in places and correspondingly slow in other places. Water is not clear anywhere. The river bottom is strong and very irregular. We have walked across the river in several places.

Second Day August 22, 1931 Al reported one cow sighted on horizon S.E. by E. at 6:45 A.M. We passed the C.N.R. Bridge at 7 A.M. The weather is more promising but wind continues to make opposition.

Another sandbar at 7:30. Man overboard at 8 A.M. Unfortunately this catastrophe came when the man concerned had his pants on and was contemplating visiting an interesting (and interested) farm lady, for the purpose of replenishing our drinking water. My partner made a suitable representation and I worked down stream.

At or about Worman an interesting looking young farmer was asked how far it was to Saskatoon. He replied. "You are going the wrong way." "Well, how far is it," I asked. Again he replied, "Hell man, you've passed the place and you'll never get there now."

Another spectator said, "It's good bye to you guys."

Third Day August 23, 1931 Last night was very unique and an excellent night for rafting. The air was calm and the heavenly bodies did all in their power to light our path. A gorgeous old moon followed us for most of the night, and the Northern Lights did all possible to help us on our way. The trip last night was almost constantly into the Northern Lights, since the river through these parts runs almost due north. We awakened this morning at 6:30 A.M. to find ourselves passing Gabriels' Ferry. We evidently passed Fish Creek during the middle part of the night. Gabriels' Ferry is 60 miles from Saskatoon.

A raft is certainly one of the simplest machines used for transportation, excelling even the wheel-barrow and stone-boat in simplicity, but the person who believes that no skill is required to successfully operate such a craft is due for a surprise or two when he travels by that means. There are certain hazards about rafting on the Saskatchewan River. The peculiar currents and many sandbars are often great hindrances. Chief among the hazards however, are the big stones, many of which are just barely covered by the water. These are the sources of greatest grief to the night traveller especially. It has been our policy on this journey to travel at all hours if weather conditions permitted. Last night we stranded several times. The most interesting experience occurred about 1 o'clock this morning when we collided with and stranded on a big rock, mostly submerged. One side of the raft stuck high and dry on the rock, while the other side was quite under the water. The old boat rocked between the angles of 20° and 30° with the surface of the water while the navigators climbed quickly from their inclined beds and endeavoured to liberate the boat.

Tiny rapids seem huge and dangerous by night and the pilot who remains on duty has strange visions of shipwreck and disaster. The night travelling therefore is less pleasant but very effective. The water is fast today and evidently higher. A skunk tried to spoil and pollute our pure fresh air of last night. The odor in our shelter became quite unpleasant and judging from the thickness of the smell, the dog which was setting up a great lot of noise on the bank was getting much the worst of the combat. Following the skunk, a heavy mist settled over the water which made it impossible to see anything on our course. The mist remained until about 6 o'clock. The scenery from Gabriels north is beautiful.

We passed Batoche at 12:30 noon (Sunday, August 23). The worst rapids experienced thus far were those on either side of Batoche Ferry. One is half a mile south and the other half a mile north of the ferry. There is an island at this point and the water on the east side of the island is quite rough and fast. The river would appear to be somewhat deeper between Haig Ferry and Batoche than between Saskatoon and Haig. The former stretch is also worse for stones.

At St. Laurent Ferry at 4:30 P.M. on Sunday. The first spruce trees are to be seen about 12 miles south of St. Louis. The travellers are still the center of considerable interest on the part of the natives. The Saskatchewan River land from Fish Creek to St. Louis is thickly populated owing to the type of land survey. Much of the land is laid out according to the old Quebec system with long narrow farms (river lots) running down to the river. Rafting on a large scale is quite new to the people we have met. They are ambitious to know where we are from and where we are going and how long we have been out of work. We are both suffering from severe sunburn today. *Monday, August 24, 1931* Progress last night was slow owing to the slow water and abundance of sandbars. The worst sandbars thus far contended are just south of St. Louis some three or four miles. There was heavy lightning and every prospect of a storm last night, but only a few drops of rain fell and this morning looks promising.

We passed St. Louis bridge at 3:45 this morning. Our craft has been officially named, "The Marna" after the most beautiful and graceful lass who ever came out of Perthshire. At 10 A.M. we found a million dead Irishmen left on a lonely and secluded sandbar.

I suggested that if I were to sing my most melodious tone that some of the natives might offer us some breakfast. The Scotch partner's observation is that they would be liable to come out with a gun and give us some buckshot. A farmer brought his team down to the water and as we came gliding by, the very unusual sight caused the team to bolt and run away. Fortunately we were out of range of the farmer by this time. Probably my partner clothed just as nature clothed him is enough to scare even a team of horses.

The sandbars from St. Louis to a point half way to Fenton are extremely bad. Progress through this part was very slow. This proportion of the river is cut up with some large islands so that the stream is frequently divided and redivided. There are a few people living in this area although farm buildings again begin to appear a few miles from Fenton. Fenton water is bad for rapids and stones. There are bad rapids 1/2 mile on each side of the ferry.

Arrived at Fenton at 2:30 P.M. and after stocking our larder we left at 3:00 P.M. Estimates re distance to Saskatchewan Forks vary from 18 to 60 miles.

The two Scotch rivermen experienced a little variation just out of Fenton some two miles. One of the rivermen thought it best to take the big rock just looming up on the right, while the other thought it best to take it on the left. As a result the raft went neither one way or the other; and in less time than it takes to tell it, the mariners were forced to work together in order to save the craft and equipment. The water was fast and deep and nothing short of a miracle saved the equipment and maybe the men. The gallon crock of water which we had just acquired left us for good, and the prophecy of one man who said we would never get back from such a trip was recalled. The bedding and other things got wet but the sun soon dried them and good spirits again prevailed. We ran until midnight when owing to many rapids, the darkness, and impending storm, we pulled our raft ashore and went to bed for four hours. The light rain and heavy thunder and lightning did us no real injury. The shelter though crude is quite effective.

Tuesday, August 25, 1931 Took the water at 4 A.M. Passed Benton Ferry at 7 A.M. Benton is 18 miles from Fenton and a mighty rough piece of water in places. As I write the rapids half a mile behind us are endeavoring to obscure the noise of the wild waters the same distance ahead of us. Between such rapids, the water is usually quite good for rafting.

We have been frequently warned about drinking the river water but our supply of fresh water was lost yesterday and we have been unable to replace it, hence the necessity of drinking what is at hand. Our food supply is in better shape. We saved all the food in yesterday's mishap and a 50¢ pail of jam purchased at Fenton is filling a great need. The fishing tackle got mixed up on the bottom of the river and is now widely separated from us. We will get no more fish. The best fishing thus far however, has been in the fish traps put out by the natives below St. Louis. At 5 or 6 o'clock in the morning the traps yielded some excellent prizes.

Last night about midnight, what appeared to be a moose came down to the water and played around sometimes drinking, sometimes just plunging. His outline was just discernible in the moonlight. The wildlife is certainly little in evidence, although the later part of the trip has displayed more than the first part. While wild ducks do not take to the river particularly readily, there are only about a dozen to be seen on the water in two days' travelling. These are the smaller kinds.

As we near Weldon Ferry the rapids become more numerous and more difficult. There are three very bad ones between Benton and Weldon Ferries. We were at Weldon Ferry at 3 P.M. From Weldon Ferry to the Saskatchewan forks is about 12 miles by water. The water in this channel is fast and deep and the rapids become more numerous and more difficult. We were at Weldon Ferry at 3 P.M. The fall of the river bed is very noticeable in places. The banks are frequently very high and covered with conifer and deciduous trees to make the scenery more beautiful than anything yet witnessed along the river. As we near the junction of the north and south rivers the stream we travel on becomes extremely winding, so much so that it appears almost to circle till it meets itself. We camp tonight under the shadow of a very high bench about one mile from the junction. The roar of the rapids will probably lull us to sleep. It is raining a little.

Wednesday, August 26, 1931 Al awakened me last night to alarm me of the fact that we had hit the shore. I reminded him that we were supposed to be there and we could trust that we would not move from it tonight. An hour later he awakened me again and hastened to say that we had drifted off and were floating down to the rapids. A kind Providence decreed that this alarm too was a fake one and again relieved, we went back to sleep.

At 6:30 we arose from our beds and climbed the highest cliff to view the country side. The Forks could not be sighted but it was certain that we were not far from them.

Arrived at the Forks at 8:30 A.M. and put ashore. My Aberdeen friend narrowly escaped a miring accident. Our equipment was transferred to the dry ground and the miry grimy victim of the mud, bathed in the river. The old raft was released and allowed to go with the stream. At first it declined to leave, appearing to prefer to linger in the still water at the shore line, but before we bade farewell to the spot, the raft moved into the current and began to drift.

The topography is very irregular and cut up in the vicinity of the junction, but also very beautiful, especially when viewed from one of the high points on the west bank.

The trip by raft is ended and we are still in the land of the living. The ten mile tramp across country to the ferry was difficult enough owing to the sunburned and sore feet and shoulders. The shoulder straps of the packs had no mercy whatever upon the raw flesh of our backs. The ten mile hike was made in about 2 hours and 40 minutes. Not bad for travellers with 25 to 30 lb. bags. We were fortunate in securing a ride from the ferry to Weldon, where we were able to get a room and a couple of man sized meals, but not before we paid in advance. With a shave (the first in a week), a hair cut, a few changes of raiment, and a hot meal, we looked and felt like artificial creatures once more.

It was a great holiday, simple, thrilling, and cheap. The entire trip and outing including cost of the raft and equipment, food, return fare by train, and incidental expenses cost the travellers just twelve dollars each.

September 1, 1931   Yesterday I came from Saskatoon to Prairie River and today Mrs. Macdonell and I drove from Prairie River to the settlement at Porcupine, some 15 miles south. This country is brand new as far as agriculture is concerned. The settlers are largely returned soldiers and families, and British families. They held their first agricultural fair here today and it was an interesting event.

The fair was held in a farmyard, with a small judging ring erected behind the stable. The first item on the judging program was a baby show. I was called upon to judge and of course objected on the grounds that it was a little out of my line. It was pointed out however, that I came there to judge the livestock and they expected me to handle the babies. I did. There were 8 entries and the contestants were held on a platform in the center of the judging ring. If it were safe to assume that the best looking mothers had the best babies, that job would be fairly easy, but evidently it doesn't work just that way. At any rate I finished the job, and had several mothers later ask me about their bodies, the eyes, health, etc.

We attended a dance in the legion hall at night and I went to roost, the guest of Mr. & Mrs. Arthur Stephenson, whose post office is Somme. I met a nice little red-headed school teacher who lives with her sister in Prairie River. The little lady is Loraine Laycock.

December 10, 1931   After an agricultural society meeting in Edenwold, I was driven over to Balgonie so that I might catch the early morning train to Regina and thence to Saskatoon. It was storming violently and I urged my kind driver to return to his home with the least possible delay after delivering me at Balgonie, while I proceeded after the midnight hour to find a bed. The only public stopping place, operated by a Chinese, was closed and the proprietor refused to get up in spite of my endeavors to break his door. He had some weeks earlier been aroused at a late hour and robbed, and he was taking no chances now. A private home was the only alternative for me and after wandering around in the blizzard, I managed to arouse the folk in a home where I was invited to stop. I had to share a bed with a fat, snoring, sweaty banker, but it was far ahead of a night in the snow.

December 24, 1931   I went home to Melfort for Christmas day. The roads are not fit for a car. Dad met me with the team and sleigh. Fat Geordie Stewart was standing on the platform when Dad and I were leaving the station. My father went up to him and said, "Geordie, I w'd like to make a trade with you." Geordie Stewart, "Allright Mac, what will you have?" Dad, "I w'd like to trade bellies with you until after Christmas."

January 17-21, 1932   My work took me to Winnipeg with a shipment of 400 finished lambs. Most of these represent the first crop of lambs from the Matador breeding experiment. They are from 8 breeds of ewes— Southdown, Cheviot, Hampshire, Suffolk, Rambouillet, Shropshire, Oxford and Leicester, and from two breeds of sires, Southdown and Cheviot. There were 16 crosses in the shipment and we endeavored to get data relative to gains, dressing %, quality of carcasses, etc.

February 27, 1932   I flagged the train at any early morning hour and came in from Elstow. The lighted lantern with which I was flagging the train went out. But I waved the gloom harder than ever and the big locomotive used its brakes.

   Spoke at the Saskatoon Herd Improvement Association meeting at noon.

   Publications of the past year:

July, 1931	The Use of Russian Thistles for Feed (Typed for distribution)
September, 1931	Protein Supplements for pigs (Mimeographed)
October 1, 1931	Oat Feed (Western Producer)
September 24, 1931	Wheat in the Pig's ratio (Western Producer)
October 1, 1931	Tanning Beef Hides (Sask. Farmer)
November 5, 1931	Tanning Hides on the Farm (Western Producer)
January, 1932	The Comparative Value of Uncut, Chaffed, and Ground Roughage for Finishing Calves. By Shaw and MacEwan (Sc. Ag.)
January 14, 1932	Slaughtering Pigs on the Farm (Western Producer)
January 21, 1932	Cutting Pork Carcasses (Western Producer)
January 28, 1932	Curing Pork Products
March 15, 1932	Methods of Curing the Meat Supply on Farm (Sask. Farmer)

Radio Talks:
November 18, 1931   The Meat Supply, CKCK, Farm School
March 5, 1932   Farm Horses and Spring Work, CKCK,
                              Farm School

Investigational Work 1931-32:
1. Protein Supplement Experiments.
2. Experiment to indicate the best use and value of pasture for Pigs.
3. Anemia in young Pigs.
4. Cross-Breeding Experiment with Pigs.
5. Study of Skeletal Structure of the Pig (ribs).
6. The use of cooked and raw potatoes for pig feeding.
7. A study of the causes of butterfat variations in dairy cows.
8. Experiments with homemade and commercial calf meals.
9. Study of the Importance of Protein level in dairy cow rations.
10. Cattle Breeding Experiment (Matador).
11. Feeding of Matador calves.
12. Market Beef Requirements.
13. The Practicability of Spaying Market Heifers.
14. Study of Value of Russian Thistle for Livestock Feeding.
15. Study of Breeds of Sheep.
16. Matador Sheep Breeding Project.
17. Breeding Experiment with Fine Wooled Sheep.
18. The Use of Commercial Oat Feed for Horses.
19. Methods of Cutting, Curing and Holding Meats and Tanning Hides for Farm Use.

Editor's Note: The selection covering MacEwan's trip to England includes only the most relevant details. He did write extensive commentaries, however, on Eskimoes and the Hudson's Bay sea route to Great Britain, not included here.

June 25, 1932   A day's work completed, and a consignment of fat cattle loaded in the cars at 8 P.M. It was my happy lot to accompany cattle reared on the old Matador ranch and finished at the University, to the big markets of the world.

While friends waited at the street of my residence, I packed a lone suitcase (with things I did not need, and left much of the other) for a two and a half months' tour. I left Saskatoon that midnight.

July 3, 1932   We stopped and rested our cattle at White River, Ontario, (the coldest place in winter, and the most beautiful in summer) for a day and a half. Roy Blake, my student assistant, and I explored and fished for the time at our disposal. We made the acquaintance of an old timer Indian who proved very interesting. I asked him his age and he replied with some little hesitation, "59 or 99, not sure which." We assured him that that was close enough.

July 6, 1932   Arrived at Montreal at 2 A.M. and got to bed at 4 A.M. We had a good run from White River and the cattle are in good order.

The cattle were roped and scissor marked today. Butcher cattle do not require to be branded or tagged.

July 7, 1932   Loaded the cattle on S.S. Manchester Division and moved off down the picturesque St. Lawrence at 10:30 A.M. The Hon. Robert Weir was the last to inspect our cattle. There are 450 cattle on board. We spent most of the day getting the cattle tied and arranged. I was made foreman over our part of the boat.

The St. Lawrence scenery is beautiful. We passed under the Quebec bridge at 10 P.M. This is not a bad trip so far, but not as attractive as a raft trip down the Saskatchewan River.

One of our passengers, a cockney whose last nickle went toward the purchase of a ticket "back 'ome" and whose farewell to Canada was, "To Hell with the land of the Maple," became ghastly seasick. At the side of the boat to which he struggled with difficulty, he parted with his last meal and both upper and lower sets of false teeth. Poor beggar was so sick he didn't care about his loss. Thought he would never need them again and hoped at times he wouldn't. An Irishman on board was very interested in the experimental cattle. He professed to know something about feeding, having worked on an experimental farm in Ireland. I questioned him about his feeding experiences—about systems of feeding, feeds, etc. and to my general question "How did you feed?" he replied, "Wet in the morning and dry at night."

July 8, 1932   Our cattle are settling down quite well. We water them at 4:30 A.M., feed hay and bed them, and repeat the job in late afternoon. The meals in the stateroom are excellent. So far I have received excellent attention. There are just two girls on board and they are not creating any great furor on account of their beauty.

We inspected the engine room. The 3 cylinder engine develops 3500 H.P. The pistons weigh 3 tons each. Fifty three tons of coal are burned daily. Propellor shaft is 200' long by 16" wide, and the speed of the shaft is 75 R.P.M.

July 9, 1932   Rain, wind and rough water. The cattle are uncomfortable, and I'm not too comfortable myself. We entered the straits of Belle Isle tonight. These straits have a bad reputation for storms, ice, fog and cold weather.

July 10, 1932   Fog all night, but we pushed along at a fair speed. It is typical of Capt. Riley to travel in spite of fog. We could see both Labrador and Newfoundland coasts this morning, and both look bleak and unattractive. We saw our first iceberg this forenoon.

My cabinmate is Jas. Rodgers, 18, of Toronto. He is a very decent kid, just out of high school and travelling to the old country for a holiday. He carries 5 grips or suitcases, and his smoking equipment includes a good supply of tobacco, large box of cigarettes and 8 pipes.

July 12, 1932   A better day. Lots of gulls following us. They tell us that these birds follow all but Scotch liners.

I reminded Blake today that some Canadian students go abroad on fellowships, and some go on cattleships.

July 13, 1932   It is interesting to get the opinion of the seamen about the Hudson's Bay Route. On the whole they regard it adversely. In the first place, ice and fog make a bad combination as experience in the Straits of Belle Isle would indicate, and secondly, the seamen say that the compass will not work north of Labrador or in Hudson's Bay. The short season, of course, is obvious, and weather may be more uncertain. The distance from Liverpool to Quebec is 2,682 miles, and to Montreal 2,822.

July 14, 1932   We have a Homing pigeon on board. There's the most wonderful example of instinct. On many trips these birds are brought across the ocean from their homes in Britain and on the return voyage, they may be released some one or two hundred miles from the home coast. They will go high, and circle, making even bigger circles, and eventually strike in the direction of home, not to rest until there.

July 16, 1932   Landed at Birkenhead at 10 P.M. The trip has been very satisfactory, lasting 9 1/2 days. The unloading process took about an hour. I had to secure special permission to disembark at Birkenhead. The boat discharges at Manchester.

July 17, 1932, Sunday   I don't know where the travelling public eats in England. There are no restaurants on the horizon. I spent the forenoon at Woodside lairage. Irish cattle have fallen off in numbers owing to the import tariff of last week. The buyers speak well of Canadian cattle and state that they are higher in quality than Irish cattle. The Irish cattle coming to Birkenhead are a low quality lot, uneven, horned and often of bad conformation.

From bitter experience I find that a hotel in this country is not a place where you can spend a night, but the sole purpose is for drinking. I have, however, at last found a hotel that deals in beds as well as bottles.

I spent this afternoon on the north side of the Mersey (Liverpool). I went through the public museum there.

The one thriving business as far as industry and commerce are concerned is "drink." It is a unique sight on Sunday evening after the "pubs" have closed until 7 P.M. to see the patrons lined up along the bar. "Smoke" is a close second in point of business importance.

July 18, 1932   Cattle offered for sale today and attracted much favorable criticism. The Shorthorn cross is favored, Hereford and Angus dividing second and third honors and Galloways fourth.

July 20, 1932   Had supper and spent the evening with Wm. L. Milne, cattle buyer and owner of one of the best retail shops in England. Mr. Milne's cousin, Kate Milne, is married to brother of Col. Potts, living in Edinburgh. Mr. Milne has an elegant home with one of the finest possible gardens, grounds, and fruit tree lay-outs.

July 21, 1932 I spent a pleasant afternoon and evening with Mr. Milne and family. They have been extremely gracious with their time and facilities. Today we toured through the most picturesque country I've ever seen. We crossed the Dee River into Flintshire, Wales, went through the towns of Buckley, Mold, Ruthin, Chester and Hawarden. The Vale of Clwyd is grandeur itself. Ruthin is an old court center for Wales. The old courthouse was built in 1401 and still stands. The church and cathedral are almost as ancient. Hawarden was the home of Wm. Gladstone. We saw a lot of Welsh country, Welsh people and Welsh livestock. All are unique and remote. The farm buildings are of ancient type and farming practises appear to be in keeping. Only livestock are kept in North Wales. Practically no grain crops grown. The Welsh sheep look very useful, the Welsh cattle (black and horned) look like overgrown Kerrys and are quite the predominant breed in the part we visited. They are dual in type but lean more to milk than beef. We saw some Welsh ponies.

July 22, 1932 I spent the forenoon at Birkenhead Market. Prices ran somewhat as follows:

Cheese	lb.	8d.
Danish bacon	lb.	6d.
Dairy butter	lb.	1s.
Loin of lamb	lb.	8d.
Fresh eggs	doz.	1s. 4d.
New potatoes	bu.	1s. 6d.
Round Beef	lb.	1s.
Leg of lamb	lb.	7d.

I found a restaurant that serves brown bread. I celebrated by eating 8 full slices for supper.

A visit to the slum district of a city like Liverpool will give one a lot to think about. The unemployment situation is not acute because the men appear to have no intention of working. Women at work are more conspicuous in certain quarters than men—they push wagons and carts, they sell papers, and raise kids in a wholesale way. The kids too are a study. They are bold, dirty and undernourished. In the poorer districts of this country, the percentage of deformed, pop-eyed, and under developed people is appalling. One wonders if the lack of restraint in such things as smoke, drink, white bread, tea and coffee, are not factors contributing to the unhappy state of child welfare.

The poor appear to have lost most of their self respect. Certainly dress and appearance play no part in this make-up. Last night I dined in state amid servants, butlers, chauffeurs, and tonight I lost myself in Liverpool's Hell. When I offered a little girl a candy if she would let me take her picture, I made a sad mistake. Shortly I was mobbed by kids and traffic was quite held up.

July 23, 1932 I partook further of the hospitality of Mr. & Mrs. Milne,

Tower Bridge, London, England.

and accompanied them into Wales. We travelled along the seacoast and passed through Chester, Colwyn Bay and Landudno. It is beautiful.

July 24, 1932 Travelled from Birkenhead to London via Chester, Newport, Wolverhampton, Walsall, Woodstock, Birmington, Stratford-on-Avon and Oxford. The single fare by bus was 15 shillings. Saw some splendid herds of Shorthorns along the way.

The bus service in Britain is wonderful. Buses travel to all parts at frequent intervals. Bus travel is cheaper than train and permits a better view of the country.

July 29, 1932 "Bonnie Scotland." Scotland is great. The country is one continuous picture, dotted with sheep, Ayrshires, and Clydesdales. It is but little wonder that such a unique country has produced the best horses, the best cattle, and the best men in the world.

As I travelled from Preston to Edinburgh last night, I saw the sun go to rest in the most beautiful setting that has yet come to my view.

Edinburgh today. The Scotsmen, and particularly the Scottish lassies, make a pleasant sort of change of scenery. I met Mr. & Mrs. Shaw. Visited Edinburgh Castle and the famous and truly wonderful National War Memorial, and the best secondhand stores in the city.

Journeyed on to Stirling where we visited Stirling Castle, the seat of the early Scottish kings and of Mary, Queen of Scots. I doubt if there is a finer view in the world than that from Stirling Castle Rock.

July 30, 1932 I am travelling now with Mr. & Mrs. Shaw. We stayed last

59

night at Perth. This morning we travelled to Dundee and then to the "granite city," Aberdeen. The feeder cattle along the road today were nearly all black polls.

This is tag day (flag day) in Aberdeen. It was on such a day in this city that Goldsmith was supposed to have conceived the germ of the poem "The Deserted Village."

July 31, 1932   Paid an early morning visit to Marna Bell, (Al Ewen's lass). Went to church and then to Jas. Durno's farm, Crichie, at Inverwurie. The Uppermill farm, once famous as the Marr farm, is 10 miles from Crichie and owned by Jas. and Leslie Durno and operated by the latter. The Shorthorns at both farms were a veritable treat. At Crichie we saw the herd bull Calrossie Engagement, a good headed, smooth topped bull, and at Uppermill we saw Garuston Commander, a good backed 2-year-old, and Glasstullick Watchman, a 3-year-old with a superb front end.

August 2, 1932   I stand tonight on the hills not far from Glen Urquart from which old Jas. Grant, son of John Grant (Ian MacIalian) came in 1773 and landed at Pictou, Nova Scotia. It is a Bonnie, gripping, wild and loveable country and surely nothing short of dire persecution would ever divorce a man from it.

Spent last night at Inverness, and conservatively speaking, it is beautiful. I climbed some high crags last night and viewed the highlands in their natural dress. This morning I visited the auction mart, saw some Highland ponies, which are a tough and hardy kind, and took the bus to Perth. Pictured Lock Vaa and some other unique Highland scenes. Came on to Glasgow and registered at the Kennilworth.

August 3, 1932   All day at the Glasgow market, dividing my attention between the dead meat market, the slaughtering activities and the livestock mart. All the livestock are sold by auction. The cattle offered were mixed in breeding, while the lambs were mostly blackfaces and blackface crosses.

Oat cakes, porridge and scones are agreeing with me much better than the English diets.

August 4, 1932   Assisted with the loading of 6 Galloway bulls billed to Saskatoon. Paid a short visit to the foreign animals' lairage where a boat load of Canadian cattle were being sold by auction. Prices ranged from 20 to 25 pounds for 1200 lb. cattle.

August 5, 1932   Travelled from Glasgow to London by night bus. I was paired off with a pretty little Scots lass and had to share my blanket with her last night.

Took train for Southampton this evening and thence to Jersey.

August 6, 1932   Arrived at St. Helier, Jersey Island this A.M. The first boat to leave Southampton last evening, and the one I tried to catch, struck some of the treacherous rocks north of the island and was reported sinking. There is a 30 to 40 foot tide on these island coasts and many dangerous reefs are laid bare at times.

Jersey Island is 12 miles long and 8 miles wide. The population is 53,000. The farms are small and the land valuable. The farms range about 15 to 20 acres in size (35 to 45 vergees). The fields are from 1 to 5 acres and usually surrounded by stone dykes or fences. Land values are from 100 to £250 per acre. Rentals run up to £25 per acre yearly. The common rotation consists of 1) grass or hay for 3 or 4 years, 2) potatoes and tomatoes or roots, 3) roots (manure after roots), 4) potatoes, 5) wheat or oats (seeded with grass). Manure is applied about once in 3 years or once in 2 years if potatoes are grown constantly. Artificial manure is used a lot.

Cattle are always tethered at pasture and are moved about 6 times daily. Conservation of grass is essential. Rye, grass and clover are the common constituents in the pastures. Cows are blanketed if the weather is cool or wet and they are stabled at night. Bulls are sometimes tethered out too, but usually not. The winter season is not severe, but some snow may fall in January and February at which time the cows will be kept in and fed hay and roots, bran and oil cake. Bran is a great favorite. Grain feed is not always given when good grass is available. They feed some bonemeal to the cows. Heifers calve for the first time at age of 2 to 2 1/2 years.

The Jersey people are most congenial. They represent a mixture of French and British. Their talk is also frequently intermediate.

I suppose here one may find the most concentrated agriculture in the world. I walked 11 miles today, and chatted all along the line, saw a lot of cows and endless picturesque scenery.

It's a funny world. I'm told on good authority that there are old women living on this island who have never seen the sea.

August 7, 1932   To an excursion trip to St. Malo, France. Had dinner at St. Malo and visited neighbouring towns and country in afternoon.

We visited Dinard Municipal Casino, one of the gayest rendezvous in this part of France. It is a beautiful building of hand-inlaid work. It houses the fashionable gambling dens, a stylish theatre, several bars and dining places, a cabaret, and a beautiful swimming pool. It is a busy place this Sabbath.

Visited St. Malo's Cafe Market, the stone wall, old castle, (St. Malo is the only walled city on the French coast) and St. Vincent's Cathedral. The cathedral is a product of the 15th, 16, 17, 18 and 19 centuries, and in it is the stone upon which Jacques Cartier last knelt before his trip to Canada.

The coast is beautiful, and Dinard is a lively city. The farms around are small, growing garden truck, apples, wheat and oats. Wheat and oats are still harvested by hand. The cattle are of mixed breeding. Veal is the all-popular meat.

August 8, 1932   Again visiting farms on the island. I have walked across the island each day out.

Mr. E.C. Perredes of Fairview farm, St. Saviours has the biggest herd on the Island, numbering 200 head. He keeps about ten stock bulls, mostly for custom breeding. The bull Brampton Beau (now sold to go to America), a strong looking chap, was bred to 900 cows in 100 consecutive days and over 800 settled to the first service and most of the balance to the second and third services. Mr. Perredes has a lot of splendid cattle and until recently, was the only man on the island using a milking machine. He likes it. Mr. Perredes judged at Toronto Royal in 1930. The two best bulls seen on his farm were Sybil's Lucky Lad, (a two-year-old, reserve champion at St. Saviours and Grouville shows in 1932) and La Pompe (a 4-year-old, second over the island in August 1931 and May 1932). Mr. Perredes seems like a good judge of cattle.

Visited the "Prince's Tower." It consists mainly of a prehistoric mound tomb constructed from unshaped rocks and covered by a huge mound of dirt. It probably dates to 3000 B.C. and perhaps beyond that. Two tombs are to be seen at the end of a long low passage. A small chapel is built on the top of the mound.

August 9, 1932   Came to Guernsey Island this morning. Peter's Port is the only city with a population of 20,000 and the entire island has about 45,000 souls. Agriculture here is much like that of Jersey. Farms are small, land prices and rentals about the same as those on Jersey. Land values range up to £400 per acre and rentals average about £8 per year. I was in several grass fields where the annual rental was £9 to £11 and the tenants are not permitted to cultivate them. About 3 grazings and a 3 to 4 ton crop of hay per acre in a year are not uncommon.

The main exports from the island are tomatoes, bulbs (narcissus, iris, tulips), grapes, vegetables, live cattle. Britain is the chief outlet for products.

I celebrated my birthday anniversary by "signing on" the "Manchester Citizen" for the return trip to Canada. Thirty minutes after the boat was due to leave, I received a wire from W.A. Wilson of London advising that I could return to Canada via Churchill (S.S. Silksworth) sailing from Newcastle August 15. I managed to get free my obligations to Manchester Lines and proceeded to Newcastle-on-Tyne. I got off the "Citizen" just as the gangplank came in and the big whistle announced to the world that the ship was departing for the new world.

Editor's Note: MacEwan was very interested in securing a passage on a ship bound for Canada via Hudsons Bay—and had solicited the Canadian High Commissioner to England to that end. His eleventh hour success was due to the efforts of the High Commissioner, a man named Wilson.

August 14, 1932   Sunday in Newcastle. Went to church once, but couldn't understand the minister.

August 15, 1932   I signed on the S.S. Silksworth at noon today and we left the dock at 3 o'clock, steaming for Churchill. Mr. Dalgaliesh thinks the practical season for the Hudson's Bay route will be August 1 to October 15. At present the route will be August 10 to October 15. At present the underwriters specify that a ship must not pass Cape Chidley before August 10. Mr. Dalgaliesh's boat, the Pennyworth, left Newcastle-on-Tyne about

S.S. Silksworth on which MacEwan travelled from Newcastle-on-Tyne to
Port Churchill on Hudson's Bay, 1932.

two weeks ago and was scheduled to pass Chidley on the opening day of
the season.

August 21, 1932   Fog and icebergs. We have been forced to stop here at
the south point of Greenland (Cape Farewell) on account of the bergs all
about us. We should have stayed clear of Greenland by 100 miles instead
of skirting Cape Farewell. Here we are in the path of the ice carried down
from the Arctic. It is carried by the current, a rebound from the Gulf Stream.

August 29, 1932   Entered the harbour first thing this morning and the
Silksworth was docked at 9:30 A.M. It is a grand sensation to put feet on
Canadian soil again.

I spent the day in exploration. We journeyed across the harbour and inspected the old fort—Fort Prince of Wales. It is a remarkable old structure
and dates back to about 1732. We also saw the old cove—sloops cove where
so many of the early settlers and explorers wintered. The rocks there bear
the names of Samuel Hearne and others. There is a picture of John Kelly,
Isle of Wight, hanging from a scaffold for stealing a goose. I found an old
Esquimau grave some distance north of the harbour.

September 2, 1932   Back to Saskatoon after a profitable and enjoyable trip
to the old land. Throughout the entire trip covering over two months, I have
scarcely retraced my steps at all. The trip was cheap because the English
pound has been down around $4.00 in Canadian money and at sometimes less.

December 13 and 14, 1932   We attempted an experiment in Rural Extension Work. I have long been anxious to give a well organized rural meat
demonstration a trial in this country. The first attempt in the province was
on February 3 and 4, 1931 when Brocklebank and I put on a Killing, Cutting and Curing demonstration on the farm of Earnie Ewing of Wisetown.

This time we went to Hanley and staged a two-day short course. The
demonstrations included slaughtering beef, pig, lamb, cutting the carcasses,

processing meats, sausage, bologna, canning, curing, rendering lard, making soap and tanning hides. The meetings which were held in a deserted garage were very encouraging. I believe that this is the most suitable type of Extension for the present time.

February 16, 1933 The Annual Agricultural Students' Association Dance. It was a nice affair. My partner was the same one as I had last year. P. Cline. (Pretty consistent.)

March 9 and 10, 1933 Short course in Melfort. The first day was given over to slaughtering. All the work was done in Keddy's Auction building which is the old Methodist Church. I would have liked a picture of Billie Wood trying to drag a Holstein steer in the front door of the old church. We killed a beef, a hog, and a lamb, and on the second day we cut the carcasses, cured and processed the meats and had an exceptionally fine reception.

I think I can claim the credit (if there be any) for starting and conducting all to date, the slaughtering and meat cutting demonstrations in this province. The first attempt was held in Wisetown (Earnie Ewing's farm) on February 3rd and 4th, 1931; the second at Hanley December 13 and 14th, 1932; the third at Swift Current February 24, 25, 1933; and the fourth one at Melfort March 9 and 10, 1933.

March 15, 1933 I was asked to speak to the Agricultural Students' Association tonight, on the Hudson's Bay Route. I did and also had the pleasure of presenting some athletic awards. At the conclusion of the meeting, the Students' Association, using John Klink as their mouth piece, very thoughtfully presented me with a white sweater carrying the college crest and an Athletic A on it. I was very happy to receive it indeed. It was in recognition of my interest and attempted help in athletics, particularly rugby and basketball.

I have coached their basketball ever since I have been here, and also the rugby team in a less official way. In the fall of 1930, the same body presented me with a gold knife carrying the college crest.

April 27, 1933 In company with Prof. Ewen, Chief of Police, Geo. Donald, and Inspector of Mounted Police, Sampson, I inspected a detachment of Mounted Police Force horses stationed in Saskatoon in anticipation of trouble with the unemployed.

Editor's Note: The reason for this inspection was not at all apparent to MacEwan. He offers no explanation beyond the fact that the Police may have wanted some official verification on the condition of their horses. He did later become an advisor to the R.C.M.P. on matters of horse breeding.

May 8, 1933 In a clash between the unemployed at the relief camp and the mounted and city police, Inspector Sampson, a promising and congenial officer whom I met on April 27th, was killed.

June 7, 1933 Before leaving Melfort, I had an interview with a delegation consisting of Mr. Codling, Jas. Gale, Dr. Dunbar, Babington, Robert Kennie. Their purpose was to offer me the Liberal Nomination for Melfort Constituency for the forthcoming Provincial election. In as gracious a manner as possible, I thanked them and explained that I preferred to continue in my present work, but upon further pressure I agreed to withhold decision for one week, at which time I would write to Robert Kennie stating finally at that time.

(Copy of letter)

902 University Drive
Saskatoon, Saskatchewan,
June 13, 1933.

Mr. Robert Kennie,
Melfort, Saskatchewan.

Dear Mr. Kennie,
   Since my return from Melfort one week ago, I have given a lot of thought to the matter which you so graciously placed before me at that time. After considering the matter from every possible angle I have decided that it would perhaps be unwise for me to sever my connections with the University of Saskatchewan at the present time. Decisions of the kind are not easy to make. If we could look into the future we might frequently reverse our decisions, but in making this decision I am endeavoring to elect the field of endeavor to which I believe I am best suited, and at the present time one which offers a generous opportunity for service to Saskatchewan Agriculture.
   Again let me say that I consider it a great honor to have been considered for the nomination and I wish to very sincerely thank you and the other members of your group. I am,

Very sincerely yours,

J.W.G. MacEwan.

July 8, 1933   At a field day at Meota. It was held right beside Jack Fish Lake on the farm of Harry Sutton. The location right by the spray from the waves was ideal for a meeting. I was the guest of Mr. & Mrs. Sutton and had a most enjoyable time. Twice I went in swimming at their point and each time I was forced to swim around the point and crawl back through the trees to where my clothes were.
August 24, 1933   A Holiday in the North
Editor's Note: Included is an account covering a walking tour in northern Saskatchewan with Dr. P.M. Simmons, a civil servant with the federal department of plant pathology
   Dr. P.M. Simmons and I left our fair city of Saskatoon at 11:30 A.M.,

bound for the wooded north. Howard Gerrie was our driver to a point south of Foxford where we strapped our packs on our backs and journeyed on foot. Our first stop was Foxford village where we were advised that one cannot get north to Candle Lake except by going west to Weirdale. Accordingly, we tramped westward some two miles and made camp by the light of the stars. A big campfire in a small bush-clearing added cheer to our chosen quarters.

Doc says it's a mistake to come into the north with low shoes—the high shoes would go much farther if one had to eat them.

We went to sleep tonight with a knife on the belt, the rifle between us, and the ax at our heads. Doc remarked that if this is a hunting trip, I'm the hunter and he is the dog. Mileage for the evening—5 miles.

August 25, 1933 Weather fine again. Country around Foxford and Weirdale is heavily wooded, with quite a few settlers of Central European type. The grain fields are few and small—mostly 2 to 6 acres in size. Log and mud houses, hand dug wells, mud ovens, good gardens with rows of poppies characterize these farmsteads.

Nightfall found us in the timber about 8 miles north of Weirdale. A serviceable teepee was constructed and we lay down before a big fire and went to sleep with the shrill howls of the timber wolves and the more familiar calls of the coyote, breaking the quietness. There are innumerable tracks of deer, elk, bear, etc. and according to the last homesteader, these animals are very numerous, beginning about the second row of sections in Township 53 Range 23.

The last house on the road or trail north (SE 34-52-23-Pat Ryan) housed a mother and father and 3 children. The oldest boy is 14 years old and has never been in school. He is a true son of the wilds and lives in a mental world of bears, elk and guns. He can climb a tree like a squirrel.

The trail north is wooded all the way, rough and rolling with frequent muskegs. Running water is not to be found after you leave the point of origin of the White Fox until you travel a township and a half north.

Doc is all in tonight. He is bent over, stiff and sore. He said, "The packsack is a fine thing but it was really intended for a horse." Mileage today—16.

August 26, 1933 It was a grand night but cool. We slept well however, and the new day bids fair.

Doc is an old man this morning. He says he wishes we could take a moving picture of him to show to any other person foolish enough to consider coming in here. "Matheson," says Doc, "Was not such a damn fool after all, when he declined the invitation to come."

The country is rare and wild and beautiful. It's great. It's certainly fine to be a millionaire and just enjoy this to the full. We found a most welcome waterhole in a muskeg between sections 22 and 23, T.53 R.23.

Our trail is very crooked and equally interesting. Every turn in the trail presents an entirely new picture. The soil is extremely variable, sand, muskeg, grey soil, etc.

We crossed the Birch Bark Creek below Torch Lake at 2:30 P.M. It is a pleasant little stream, full of stones and clear water. I caught one fish in it. The trail to Candle leads east of Torch Lake and is most indirect. We passed a lot of old Indian graves and mounds.

The drinking water problem has been baffling on this journey. Plenty of low marshes, but practically no running water. Not a settler from SE 34-52-23 to Candle Lake by our route.

Doc is tired and disgusted. He says there is a packsack for sale cheap when he gets back to Saskatoon. We met one man moving in from Chaplin, Saskatchewan with two loads of effects. This wild, desolate country looks good to him. His name is Stevens. Arrived at Candle Lake at 7 P.M. It is a beauty spot. Mileage for day—15.

August 27, 1933 We took possession of a log cabin situated on the narrows between Torch and Candle last night. Contrary to Doc's advice, the door of the cabin was left open when we retired and at a late hour, a big black form appeared in the doorway. It was either a bear or a dog, and certainly the former are more numerous in these parts. The evening prior to retiring was pleasantly spent around a campfire with a trapper Fred Clavelle, who wandered along. He was good enough to join us in conversation and after considerable priming, he told some of the inside stories about the north country. Fred Clavelle is a French Canadian and has trapped in New Brunswick, Ontario, Manitoba and Saskatchewan for 20 years. The business in recent years has offered only a lean existence. His season begins in the White Gull country northeast of here on October 20 and lasts until early February. Last winter's catch gave him only $300 worth of furs, while $2,000 was an average return some years ago. He is starting to take his supplies in to his cabins (4 of them) now and carries a pack of 75 to 100 lbs. He has 4 cabins on a 60 mile trap line. Wolf, fox (Red and Cross), coyote and weasel are his principal victims now. He tells many interesting tales about being tracked and followed by timber wolves, chased by a bull moose, etc.

Candle Lake consists of a store and 4 modest cabins. The population at present comprises 4 men and 3 women. Eight trappers make Candle Lake their headquarters, but they are mostly out in the wilds or elsewhere just now. The fish camp 3 miles northwest along the lake has a few residents and has seen some busy times in past winters. Whitefish are caught in large numbers in the winter months.

Candle Lake is beautiful. The south shore is nearly all sanded and wooded. Hills rise on the north side of the lake, and incidently there is a big bush fire raging north today. The land north of Candle Lake is poor, sandy, ridges and muskeg, and offers little or nothing for farming.

I had the misfortune to tear a 12-inch gash in my trousers while walking through the woods. The matter was fairly well corrected when I sewed it up with jack knife and a piece of white string.

There are a couple of excellent gardens here at the Candle Lake settlement. Garden corn, ripe tomatoes, vegetable marrow, celery and other common vegetables are to be found in the Hanson garden. There has been no frost at this point to date, although frost has been reported at Paddockwood and some other points south of here.

August 28, 1933 We spent the day exploring north and east. I journeyed east of the lake in search of bear but was rewarded only with a glimpse of one in the thick bush. I spied a couple of big game in the distance. Mr. Van Owen, who came in here last December from Nipawin, got a bear yesterday, and I was presented with a generous supply of bear steak. It tasted fine, a little like pork although dark in color.

I climbed the ranger's tower on the east side and got what was positively the finest picture I ever laid my eyes upon. The Candle is the pick of all the lakes I have ever seen in Canada and the pretty little Torch and Bay Lakes lying close by make the picture complete.

I helped Mr. Van Owen to tan his bear skin. Mr. Van Owen does a little trapping, picks berries, and raises a few mink. He has just had the mink a short time, but they seem to give good promise.

The bush fire on the north looks very bad.

Had a swim in the Candle.

I returned to the ranger's tower tonight, climbed its 76 feet and again feasted upon the grandeur of nature, nature at her best. It was at sunset and only the kind that is seen in the north. The two mile walk through the bush by dark was frought with visions and forebodings. It is easy to hear bears, see bears and fairly feel bears when walking through the bear territory at night.

Mr. Gurney is the storekeeper at this point. His business is not heavy, but it doesn't take much to keep these folk.

August 29, 1933 Mr. Gurney rowed us to the west side of Torch Lake and we were on our way toward Paddockwood.

One thing that strikes me about this frontier country – those who are here would consider living at no other place. It is their choice and though they seldom see any of the complications of modern society and convention, they are very happy.

Candle Lake takes its name from an old Indian legend about a light that was seen over the waters. We are told that the Indians to this day will not go on the lake and will not be found near the shoreline at night.

The good land extended from the landing on the west side of Torch Lake for nine miles on the trail toward Paddockwood. We had dinner at the ranger's tower about 9 miles S.W. of the Landing. From the tower there is poor land and Jack Pine for another 9 miles. We camped tonight at Howard's Creek, 15 miles from the Landing and 9 miles from Paddockwood. We hit along at a good pace today on account of the scarcity of water along the route. We drank of the natural beverage at Iron Springs 3 1/2 miles from the Landing, and again at a muskeg where we dug a hole with a hatchet and squeezed water from the mud into a cup. It was black and grimy, but it was nonetheless, the most welcome drink I can recall. Our third drink was at Howard's Creek where we camped for the night. We got a few blueberries along the way today.

August 30, 1933   Our camping site on the edge of the Howard Creek was 100% last night. It was comfortable, and the log bastion which we erected gave our sleeping quarters a measure of security and protection from wandering elk. The elk are rutting now and consequently they are not congenial to meet or know.

There has been a small forest fire along Howard Creek these last two days but the fire gang has it well under control today. Howard Creek is 10 miles from Paddockwood.

If I ever have a fortune to leave, a portion of it will be designated for the erection of a suitable memorial to "The Pioneer's Horse." The poor brute should be recognized in some lasting way. The memorial should depict an old thin horse, in crude flimsy harness, his head down, and ribs projecting visibly from his sides. The world will never know what these brutes have suffered from privation, long hauls and bogs.

We walked 10 miles this forenoon and got into Paddockwood at 10:30 A.M.

The characters along the way and in the village are very interesting. We picked up an old trapper and hunter on the road this morning. He came from "Minisotee" and if he can trap and hunt as well as he can swear, he should do well.

The unsettled wilds are now pretty well behind us. They are most interesting and refreshing. There is great individuality about the inhabitants, about every mile of the road. Even the equipment used in that new land is unique. I think of the horse and the bull that were hitched together and hauling hay for Mr. Cronk who lives near Iron Springs, on this side of the Torch Lake. The poor old bull deserves a memorial too. There is one of the finest examples of frontier efficiency. He works all day, he is used for breeding purposes at times, and when he has outlived his usefulness he will be slaughtered and eaten. He deserves some recognition.

August 31, 1933   We caught the train at Paddockwood and arrived home at Saskatoon at 11 P.M., dirty and whiskered, but convinced (speaking for myself only) that the north country is a kindly country for a resourceful man.

It was a cheap trip, everything including car and train transportation and food for the week cost less than $9.00. Unless my ravenous appetite subsides however, I may be forced to conclude that the trip was costly.

September 18, 1933   The grasshopper damage this past season has been very serious in certain southern Saskatchewan areas. There is prospect for a more serious infestation next summer. The Agricultural workers of this city and district were called together today to hear Ken King of the Dominion Entomology Branch station here, give his views on the situation. An enthusiastic campaign is being organized at once.

September 25, 1933   Upper years enrolled at the University. Contrary to expectations, the enrollment does not appear to be markedly down.

Farming "Farming is a messy business—so uninteresting—and cows . . ."
So said one whose chief pleasures in life are choir practises, bridge parties, golf and late nights. Perhaps farming is like that somewhat, but it's pretty much in the way you look at it.

Hasn't it been that vocation which has made men, provided leaders, and imparted the best judgment and foresight to leaders in finance, administration, politics and other walks of life?

Granting that farming is fraught with certain hazards and hardships, one may refuse to take the least stock in the theory that it is uninteresting. As one who was born and reared on the farm, knows something of its hardships, of pioneering and privation, the writer may advance the contention that the city dweller has no monopoly on the interesting things in life.

It is unfortunately true that some farming folk are not getting all they should out of their work. Their work is irksome, tedious, monotonous and unfruitful to them. Perhaps they have always been too close to that work to obtain the happiest picture, so close to the work in the fields that it has meant only long hours and heavy toil, so constantly close to the cow that she means only manure to fork and teats to pull. There are compensations on the farm which are frequently under-rated. The joy of working as a partner with nature in her great laboratory, and the joy of caring for living animals which are growing, yielding and responding to the skill of the operator are compensations of no mean caliber. The compensation of hunger is food, the compensation of thirst is water, and of fatigue—rest. It can scarcely be questioned that there are some city dwellers who do not know the great joy of eating because they are never hungry, and they don't know the real joy of sleeping because they have not had sufficient experience with real toil. The finest compensations in the writer's life were not the circuses visited, theaters attended, or bridge parties endured, but rather the simplest compensations of natural life. The long drink of cold, grimy, soot-colored water which was squeezed from the muskeg mud after a nine mile walk under a 30-pound pack and an August sun was the most welcome draught ever to come to the writer's lips. It was liquid which the average person would not consider washing his feet in, but under the circumstances, it was so cheering, refreshing, and reviving that the pleasant thought of it will remain long after the outstanding social events of city life are forgotten.

It may still be contended that a cow is beautiful, that food to a hungry man is sweet, that water to a thirsty man is the most welcome thing in the world, and a good bed to a tired man is the nearest approach to Heaven itself. It may be contended too that for those souls who find nature more interesting than contract bridge, the farm holds broader understandings of the way of life, finer appreciation of things and fellows, and the most genuine of compensations. There are those who can sincerely say with one Saskatchewan farmer (Frank Richardson) "There is nothing more pleasant for me than to do chores on my own farm.''

Written in church October 22, 1933
J.W.G. MacEwan

Editor's Note: The fact that this section on farming was written in church could well give an insight into MacEwan's re-evaluations of his church-going practices and attitudes. As he was prone to admit in later life, the formalized church seemed to be offering less and less as the years went by.

November 7, 1933 Aunt Martha Grant died at Tisdale Hospital. She had been operated on for appendicitis some weeks ago. She died of a stomach hemorrhage, presumably not related at all to her operation. She was 71 years old. Funeral will be at Zion Church, North Brandon on November 10th.

November 15, 1933 I spent the evening with Uncle John Grant who is returning from his wife's funeral at Brandon. He will go home to St. Louis tomorrow. He went to St. Louis and took up his present land in 1921 in which year he borrowed 4 horses from us at Melfort. He got Old John, Prince, and the two broncho mares. Uncle John came to Manitoba in 1879 and to Brandon in 1880. He is one great character—not handsome, looks like a hard working, simple living man, and he is; but he has a wealth of character, generous and quiet. If all our people were of his type, there would be neither wars nor depressions. I regard Uncle John Grant as the ideal Canadian citizen.

November 21, 1933 Mr. W. of Fort Qu'Appelle, Saskatchewan has owed us some money for quite a long time. His recent death was rumored. Being unable to obtain reliable information locally, I put in a long distance phone call to the man and the operator, after doing all in her power, advised me that the other party had died. Do you wish to cancel the call? I told her she might do as she thought best, if she still thought she could communicate by phone with him, it would be all right with me, otherwise cancel the call.

November 25, 1933 I am on crutches tonight. I have been coaching the Agricultural College basketball team and at the conclusion of the practise this evening I shot for a basket, took the rebound and attempted a backhand shot in mid-air. I came down on a twisted ankle and it certainly fixed me for a while. I had been feeling very sorry for myself at the discomfort of limping slowly to wherever I had to go. Tonight I limped at snail's speed to College building and found that I was travelling just ahead of a little girl who has never walked any faster and never will. Guess I've a lot to be thankful for.

December 7, 1933 It wouldn't be a University Dining Hall if the students didn't criticize the food. One of the boys said today that he didn't mind eating horse, but he did wish they would take off the harness. The beef was tough.

On my return from the Old Country in September, 1932, I was offered $3.00 for a pound note I had left. Today the same bank gave me $5.00 for it. I vowed I would never let them have it for 3.

December 12, 1933 Mother prepared a noon meal which might well have been a Christmas dinner, with turkey and all the accessories. Two meetings at Melfort this afternoon and evening. This afternoon I talked to the Shorthorn Breeders Club on "Breeding" and tonight I talked on British Agriculture, Overseas Markets, and Hudson's Bay. Owing to bad roads and severe weather the meetings today were not large.

December 25, 1933   Mother and Dad disappointed me by not coming down for Christmas. I spent the day quietly reading "Forgotten Men," a new book. Had a short skate in the afternoon and went to Mr. F.M. Riche's home for evening meal. There were food and drink in abundance.

December 31, 1933   The year 1933 ends amid unhappy scenes. Trouble has loomed large in 1933. It was the 5th year of the depression which has not yet released its grip. Poverty, unemployment, famine, drought and grasshoppers featured the year. The International political arena has been equally unsettled, with war talk in Europe and in South America and the Orient. We welcome the new year with high hopes.

January 1, 1934   Miss Jerry Stormont and I attended the Watch Night service in St. John's Cathedral last night. It was very nice and certainly a great improvement on the manner some elect to see the new year in.

January 6, 1934   What a great sense of independence a little property gives one! Today I own the bed I sleep in – bought it and a small table from Prof. Murdo Matheson for $10.00.

January 9, 1934   I am evidently conspicuous in the mornings by the large plate of porridge I consume, but that's all right. When one has had a large ration of porridge, it tends to change his whole outlook on life. It fairly makes one think the depression was over.

January 19, 1934   Tonight my father and I took in a talking moving picture. It was the first "talkie" my father had seen.

January 21, 1934   Have just completed reading Scott's "Rob Roy." Think I'll call my first son Rob Roy MacGregor MacDonald MacEwan.

January 25, 1934   Robbie Burns night. I attended the banquet, concert and dance and came away with the idea firmly fixed in my mind that Robbie Burns was the finest man the world has produced and that all Scotsmen are superior beings. I attended the banquet with Al Ewen. Rev. Abernathy from Melville was the principal speaker.

January 25, 1934   The chairman at the Burns Dinner explained that everything that was in a haggis came out of the sheep. Some of his listeners misunderstood and thought he said that everything that was in a sheep went into the haggis.

February 4, 1934   The first meeting of the proposed Qu'Appelle House Forum was held in my room this Sunday afternoon. The first turnout, though not large, was very encouraging. Our proposal is to meet every Sunday afternoon to discuss International problems and events of world for the current week. We first of all outlawed three topics; economics, politics, and student problems, hoping that we can get down to something more concrete than these topics would permit.

February 11, 1934 This morning I had more than average difficulty remaining awake in church. I came out of a doze with a start and looked up to see Rev. Orton's finger at arm's length pointed at me and the Rev. gentleman looking right at me. I felt his challenge, but don't know yet just what it was.

We ate and discussed Roquefort cheese at the Qu'Appelle House Forum. Some of the boys had never tasted it before. It was suggested that with a selling price of 85¢ lb., it was too bad we couldn't make it in Canada instead of importing it from France. Tommy Fraser, who had regarded it with considerable suspicion, said, "I don't suppose Canada is an old enough country to have cheese like that."

February 25, 1934 As I sat in Knox Church this morning I was reading Hymn No. 264, "Strong Son of God Immortal Love, Whom we that have not seen Thy face, By Faith and faith alone embrace, Believing what we cannot prove," when Mrs. S. rose to contribute a solo. Perhaps the solo was very fine and perhaps appreciated—I don't know, but to me the verses of the hymn and the solo contrasted sharply. The former had depth, meaning and reality, the latter tingled with emptiness and echoed meaninglessly.

March 27, 1934 The Agricultural College basketball team which I have had under my direction this winter, was tonight crowned undisputed inter-faculty champion.

April 2, 1934 Supper at Ewen's tonight. Two boiled eggs, bread and butter and corn syrup. Ewen is a great cook.

April 10, 1934 I attended a meeting of the local board of directors of the British and Foreign Bible Society. I was elected to that board beginning of this year.

April 11, 1934 An interesting, simple and pleasant evening. My first evening visit was to the Kirk home. Mr. Kirk is very sick, but in spite of his 80 years and his failing heart, he is the essence of cheer. He remarked that the city is a bad place for him, he wants to go to his son's homestead at Meadow Lake. His has been a long and Christian life, and until this recent sickness Mr. Kirk had the mind and physical activity of an average man of 60.

Visit No. 2 was to Mr. & Mrs. Hallodilloff who live on Avenue J. This is their Easter season and their table tonight was decked with many Russian dishes including "Baba," a yellow cross between bread and cake, and "Pasha" or Easter cheese. The latter is a rich cottage cheese containing yolk of eggs, vanilla, raisins, etc. Mrs. H. escorted me to an anteroom in which she had her potted plants and flowers. She is proud of them and she said, "This is my Maskota." I learned that Maskota means "for happiness," but evidently has no exact parallel in English.

As I sat down to supper she said, "Professor MacEwan, I hope you are very angry." She repeated and then Mr. H. drew her attention to an error and after a moment of conversation with her husband, she apologized and hoped that I was very hungry, not angry.

The Hallodilloffs are refreshing old people of a splendid type. They are generous to the limit, they have excellent taste and the old man has a unique respect for the feelings of animals.

April 12, 1934   Mrs. Brenton, mother of Miss Brenton (steno. in Extension Dept.) was 89 years old today and had a birthday party. I was there. I poured tea for a part of the time. No dishes broken. All marvelled at my grace and charm in pouring.

Mr. Bell of the Provincial Income tax office, Saskatoon, was at the party and reminded me of my threat of one year ago when paying my tax, that "before another year went by I would have a wife and twins and I'd fool the income tax department." I asked Mr. Bell for another year in which to work.

May 1, 1934   An old timer in the Elrose district told us of hauling water for his oxen 7 miles in the early days. He would put three barrels on the wagon, hitch the bulls and drive to the spring. He would fill the barrels two-thirds full and at least one barrel of water would be lost on the way home, and when he had given the two oxen a drink, no water remained and it would be time to go for more water. The oxen would never drink at the spring, but would take their fill when they arrived home.

May 11, 1934   Convocation exercises at Third Avenue United Church. 233 students received degrees and 144 got certificates. Sir Frederick Haultain, chancellor of the university, gave the Address and by virtue of its shortness, was the most popular convocation address in years.

At the Graduation dance until happy to come home.

Editor's Note: Frederick Haultain was the political driving force behind western efforts to gain provincial status for Alberta and Saskatchewan in 1905. In this sense he might be described as a founding father of modern western Canada. Predictably, MacEwan held Haultain in very high esteem.

May 27, 1934 (Sunday)   This is Rural Sunday at the Hughton and Elrose United Churches. I came out to Rosetown by train last night and was met there by Rev. Norman Campbell, minister at Elrose. I am staying at the simple and wholesome home of the Campbells. Today I gave the address at both Hughton and Elrose church services. My address was an attempt to discuss Agricultural, Social and Religious problems of the rural people, placing each in its proper relationship.

June 8, 1934   Writing a letter to a dying man is not easy. I wrote this evening to George Hassan (BS Guelph and MS Saskatoon) who is dying in St. Joseph's Hospital, Sunnyside, Toronto, from cancer of the pancreas. Poor old George has had far more than his share of trouble. A refugee from Russia, lost his wife in the struggle, and not a kind that could ever fit in in Canada as he would like. He took Master's work in Animal Husbandry, finishing in 1932 with us.

June 13, 1934   Had the interesting experience of meeting a dark-eyed girl, *Patricia La Blanc* of Regina on the train. She had just this morning been released from a six months' term at the Battleford Women's Jail on a forgery count. Her stories of jail and life were most interesting and Regina came all too soon. I realized, perhaps more than ever before, what an awful ordeal such a sentence must mean.

June 19, 1934   Overwhelming victory for Liberal Party in the Saskatchewan Provincial elections today. Five C.C.F. elected, *no* Conservatives and the balance (49) Liberals. Estey and Norman were the successful candidates in Saskatoon, and Premier Anderson and Hon. Howard McConnell were defeated.

Beer plebiscite gave "beer by the glass" a majority.

Liberals 49 — C.C.F. 5 — Conservatives 0.

June 27, 1934   1.45'' of rain fell last night. That was the heaviest single fall since September 12, 1931. Already, this June is the wettest since June 1928. Growth is good, although grasshoppers are still capable of doing great harm. The grasshoppers are worst in the memory of the present generation, but the weather thus for has been against them.

July 10, 1934   Left Saskatoon this afternoon with Mr. Stan Vigor, Field Crops Commissioner and Mr. Hedley Auld, Deputy Minister of Agriculture for Saskatchewan, and drove to Melfort. We arrived at Melfort at 9 P.M. after having supper at Birch Hills. We were advised on our arrival at Melfort that a hailstorm and hurricane had just subsided and that crops from Pathlow to Ridgedale were ruined. Our farm was in the path of the storm and the plots which were to be the central feature for tomorrow's field day at Dad's farm are also a complete loss. The field day to which we were coming is cancelled.

I took Mr. Auld's car out toward home tonight, but slid off the road near Bert Robson's and spent the night at his place.

July 11, 1934   A few people gathered at the farm in spite of field day cancellation. Mr. Auld and Mr. Vigor and I spoke. The country which had an outstanding crop is today a wreck. Buildings were torn and upset and trees uprooted and broken. The storm of yesterday was on the same day (July 10) as the one which cleaned us out in 1919.

July 14, 1934   Some unused moments in the evening were devoted to a rolling pin throwing competition for the women. They were obliged to throw overhand at their husbands, who were allowed to stand as far away as they thought necessary. It was a great success and 15 women participated. I take the credit of introducing rolling pin throwing competitions in Saskatchewan. Mrs. Ralph Tompkin was first with a distance of 57 2/3 feet, and Mrs. Alex Bradford was second.

August 13, 1934   Armed with a rifle, frying pan, ax, blanket and food, which included about half a peck of oat-cakes (5 dozen to be exact), Al Ewen and I left Saskatoon for the north country. We were fortunate in getting a ride with Jack Rayner as far as Paddockwood, which is practically the north limit of passable auto roads. Shouldering our packs which weighed a little over

25 pounds each, we walked on toward Candle Lake and camped for the night one mile north of the muskeg on the Weirdale road. It looked like a wet night, but the tent afforded all the protection necessary, and apart from the howl of wolves, we were undisturbed.

August 14, 1934   Arose from our pine-bow beds at 4:30 and were on the trail at 5:30. We visit for a brief interval at the new home of W.B. Stephens and family on S.E. 24, 54, 23, 8. They came in from Chaplin, Saskatchewan where they had five successive crop failures. They came in last fall and are well established now. They have horses, cattle, five sheep and some fitch. Mr. Stephens is quite optimistic about sheep for this part. The Stephens put up 150 quarts of wild raspberries and some quarts of other wild berries. The father and four sons have taken homesteads and they say they like the country. To date they have 5 acres broken and their land looks very good. They have this to say, that if a man brings his equipment with him, he can almost live off the country.

It appears that willows are growing on the best land, while poplar land is next best, then spruce and lastly Jack Pine.

We passed the new log house in process of completion of J. Kolenko, on N.W. 30-54-22.

We arrived at Candle Lake at 10:30 A.M. after walking 15 miles already this day. The lake looks as absolutely lovely as ever.

We negotiated a Scotch deal with Mr. T. Hanson, an old timer here, for a boat that might be a cross between a canoe and a parent of unknown denomination. The price paid was $5.00 and at 12:30 noon, we left Candle Lake Portage and later in the afternoon entered the mouth of the Torch River down which we hope to paddle.

It is worthy of note that Mrs. Hanson's garden is as good as can be seen anywhere. There is no evidence of frost yet. They had home-grown cucumbers on August 5th and will have corn next Sunday. Mr. Hanson's message to the people outside is, "We need a road."

Our boat leaks a little, but promises to be useful. We successfully navigated a series of rapids about 7 or 8 miles from the mouth of the river and three miles further, quite bad rapids gave cause for special caution. We travelled tonight until 8:15 and made camp on a beautiful Jack Pine site high over the water.

August 15, 1934   Up at 5:30, breakfasted and left the camp at 7 o'clock. Evidently we underestimated our appetites on this trip, because prospects already suggest a food shortage. We made one meal today on wild duck. The big game seems plentiful. An elk visited us early this morning and later in the day we had perfect view of three moose including one calf.

The river this morning was ideal for boating although rapids were numerous this afternoon. A near mishap occurred when we passed under a fallen tree, leaving Al suspended and half filling the boat with water.

Our boat has been christened "the S.S. Phyllis" because it is very hard to control.

The scenery continues beautiful. It surpasses anything I have ever seen in Canada. The trip, thus far has been one continuous feast of beauty. We camped tonight at the foot of noisy rapids.

August 16, 1934   Food supplies uncomfortably low. Al anticipates eating our fish bait if no relief comes shortly. Today we had oat-cakes for breakfast, sardines and bread for dinner and bacon and bread for supper.

Wildlife is abundant on and along the river. We were quite close to a mink this morning. The river banks are marked everywhere by the feet of big game.

Rapids galore this morning, and this afternoon a lazy and crooked river. The loops were regular, and for several hours progress was negligible. With the threatening food shortage and the non-appearance of a landmark where we thought we might get food, our patience was being tried. When Al complained bitterly, I reminded him of the patience old Columbus must have displayed and how he, each day, made the same entry in his log-book— "This day we sailed on." Al's reply was "Yes, but Columbus wasn't as damn near out of food as we are."

This evening we encountered a dam on the river, made by fallen trees and drift. It was wide and formidable and we were obliged to portage. It was an awkward situation with the miry mud threatening to engulf us when we lifted our cargo. Made camp tonight at 8 P.M.

August 17, 1934   This is our fourth day on the Torch River. It rained quite heavily early this morning so we did not rise until 8 o'clock. The rapids have been many and bad enough throughout the day, but we are congratulating ourselves upon the skill which we now have in navigating the roughest water.

The scenery has continued unbeatable. One cannot help but love this wild, unoccupied country. The conifers are numerous and at times, line both banks. I have thought so often today of the hymn, "Peace perfect peace, in this dark world of sin." It all contrasts so obviously with the environment we labor in day by day. It is good for one's soul to get away from dishonest men and silly women. "When peace like a river, surroundeth my soul."

We consumed the last of our food and camped tonight still beyond the fringe of settlement, with semi-empty stomachs. The rapids this evening were very bad, but we managed to travel until dark without mishap.

August 18, 1934   Rain again last night. We arose and were on the water at 4 A.M. One hour later we arrived at Jacob's Mill where the turbulent waters almost engulfed us. It was a coincidence that the moment we were landing to leave the river, our old boat, which could stand the strain for which it was never intended no longer, filled with water and sank, and gave us a ducking.

There is a curious difference in hospitality shown as one travels around. Yesterday a trapper gave us the last half loaf of bread he had and refused to take payment for it, and today, when we called at Jacob's Mill, we offered to trade our boat for two sandwiches to curb our hunger. The man to whom we were talking could not be bothered. "Hell, I've just got up and I can't do anything for you." We thanked him for the hospitality he might have shown but didn't. Perhaps our appearance was not in our favor. A week's growth of beard and wet, tattered clothes do make one look different. Incidently, the seat is almost entirely missing from my pants. Rebuked by our fellow human, we turned down the trail, and stopped to make a meal of blueberries. We walked seven 1/2 miles south to the railroad just out of White fox and there caught the train going to Prince Albert.

It is disappointing to have to mingle once again with humans. They are such an unstable lot. Went into a store in Prince Albert to buy a paper. The clerk turned to the customer whose face was covered with whiskers and said, "What do you want?" Later in the evening, after a good shave, the same clerk approached the same customer with, "Yes sir, what can I do for you?"

Stayed last night at Merchants Hotel.

November 29, 1934 Bedford Road Collegiate is the scene of a basketball tournament open to city teams. The Old Boys, also known as the Grads, who have not been out together for several years, entered and won the evening game against College of Agriculture. With the Grads' team were Harry Puller, Mat White, Balfour Kirkpatrick, Ray Frey, Colb McEwen, Roy Blake and myself.

November 30, 1934 It was my lot to attend a reception given for a travelling violinist in whom I had no interest. The whole episode was ghastly to say the least. The hour was late, the people stiff and all in evening dress, no place to sit down, and a lot of silly females adorned with drugstore faces. I am surprised at myself at being seen at such a place, but such seems the price of what we regard as modern civilization.

December 2, 1934 Won our fourth and last game against Bedford 27-54. We now have the Bedford tournament championship.

December 11, 1934 Mr. Harry Littlecrow, red man from the Whitecap reserve, visited me today. Harry doesn't smell too well, but he is a well built mixture of red and white and he has a lot of good sense. He had a lot of good things to say for my Indian relics, notably the bone scalping knife and the old flintlock. He tells me the best bone knives were made from the jawbone of an antelope. Harry is a Sioux.

January 1, 1935 I have resolved to abstain from tobacco and coffee in 1935. I celebrated this New Year's day by attending the Prince Albert Mintos vs Saskatoon Standards hockey game, at the Stadium. It took an overtime period to make the score 3-2 for Mintos.

January 20, 1935 On behalf of Tommy Shaddick, who is clinging rather feebly to life in the City Hospital, I was introduced to the operation of blood transfusion. The operation is not a serious one but as one is prostrate on the operating table and doctors and nurses are buzzing about, the thing appears about as serious as a leg amputation. They took about 550 c.c. of blood from me. My blood type "Group 4," (universal donor group). After the operation I walked from the City Hospital to the Ross block on 3rd Avenue, "without brandy." A little Highland Scots blood should do the recipient a lot of good.

January 21, 1935 Tommy Shaddick died early this morning.

January 23, 1935 No relief from the severe weather. Tonight we attended a banquet in the Saskatchewan Hotel. It was followed by addresses by Premier Bracken and Hon. Gordon Taggert, and then a dance. The supreme of loveliness was Patricia Starr with whom I managed to have 4 dances.

February 23, 1935 I was named official chaperone to a dance in our gymnasium last night and clean forgot about it. I went to bed and heard nothing until I was reprimanded this morning.

March 7, 1935 To Yorkton for Agricultural Short Course. I find in travelling by train if I can make the acquaintance of the prettiest girl or the toughest looking man on the train, the time will pass quickly. Today I managed to win the confidence of a half-breed chap, Henry Campeau, of Archerwell. Upon questioning him, I learned that he was born on the reserve at Rose Valley. I mentioned going through Rose Valley on one July evening last summer with Mr. Hedley Auld and intending to stop at that town for the night, but finding that the town was wrapped in excitement, there having been a stampede that day, we moved on. I also mentioned to my acquaintance that when I was there, a fight between a white man and an Indian was just about to begin. He said "I was the Indian."

April 10, 1935 Knox Church Men's Banquet. The pie was excellent (I consumed half a pumpkin and 1/4 an apple pie) and the programme good. The Salvation Army boys stole the honors with a coronet solo and trombone quartet.

April 13, 1935 Dr. Murray's annual dinner to the retiring student executives and those members of the faculty associated with them. Jack Jones, the incoming president of the S.R.C., expounded his famous elephant theory tonight. He said handling women was just like handling elephants. You put a rope around the neck, find out which way they want to go and hang on.

June 9, 1935 Al Ewen and I sun-bathed this morning. It was not until I was at morning church service that I realized that my pants must have been on an ant mound while I was tanning my hide. Ants would be excusable in church if they would not insist on spending most of their time on their victim's neck. To contribute to my distraction, one which I removed from my hide climbed up on the lady ahead of me and spent a few busy minutes playing around and dodging her efforts to dislodge it from her neck.

June 30, 1935 Phyllis and I decided finally to get married about July 26.

July 25, 1935 Announced livestock parade before grandstand tonight. Dad came into the city for tomorrow's affair. Mother is in Melfort hospital and will be unable to be with us.

July 26, 1935 Phyllis Cline and Grant MacEwan were wed. The place was the Saskatoon Forestry Nursery, the day was excellent and Dr. John Nicol officiated. About 50 people were present, among them, Hon. Robert Weir, who just arrived from Ottawa today. Phyllis and I left at 5 P.M. amid a small hurricane of excitement and devilment. To Rosetown by train.

Editor's Note: Phyllis Cline's uncle Jim Maclean was Superintendent at the Forestry Nursery. John Nicol was another relative of Phyllis and held a doctorate in theology. MacEwan's best man was Al Ewen, while the bridesmaid was Esther Sutherland, a school friend of Phyllis'.

The bride's gown was plain white satin with cowl neck, train, and full length veil.

Robert Weir was a friend of the MacEwan family and was currently Minister of Agriculture in the federal cabinet. Phyllis recalls two anecdotes of the wedding. Before the wedding when both bride and groom are traditionally not in public view, MacEwan stood at the entrance effusively greeting all guests until ushered away by Al Ewen. Then following the reception, which was also held at the Nursery, the newlyweds' departure for Saskatoon was delayed because the groom could not be found. After much searching, he was located in the parking lot, helping a guest change a flat tire.

September 3, 1935 Moved to our new abode, 1939 Elliott, the upper part of Mrs. MacCallum's duplex home. We will pay $45.00 per month for November, December, January, February and March and $40 for each of the other months.

October 1, 1935 My father was taken to Melfort Hospital for an operation for both hemorrhoids and an abdominal rupture. The operation was serious enough and very painful. Three weeks was the stated minimum for his stay after the operation but on election day, October 14th, the doctor acceded to the request that he be allowed to vote. Dr. McHendry drove him to the valley and after voting, the doctor was going to take him back to the hospital, the old Scot said,"No chance, I'm out and out I'm staying." He went home.

October 8, 1935 Meeting of the Saskatoon Archaeological Society, College Building, and Dr. Morton was the speaker—topic—Migrations of the Tribes. We will some day regard A.S. Morton as one of Canada's genuinely great historians.

Editor's Note: This is MacEwan's first reference to Arthur Silver Morton, Professor of History at the University of Saskatchewan, and a leading authority on western Canadian History. His monumental *History of the Canadian West to 1870* still stands today as the standard reference work in the field.

December 12, 1935 Agricultural Society meeting at Paynton. This evening George Wyatt and I were guests of Captain Black at his farm 1 1/2 miles east, but before we got there, we were in an exciting run-away, from which I jumped and George Wyatt was thrown, receiving several minor injuries. My buffalo coat saved me from injury when I jumped and rolled a few times on the hard road.

December 31, 1935 With the completion of the old year, Ewen and I finished the first part of our proposed "Canadian Feed Unit" feeding standard. We have spent many late nights on it. It has been midnight each night this week. **Editor's Note:** MacEwan had noted the lack of prescribed tables for rationing and regulating the food intakes of animals. He felt that the American standards were not always compatible with the Canadian and thus set out to compile a Canadian standard. This Standard was published in the Appendices of MacEwan and Ewen's first book, *Science and Practice of Canadian Animal Husbandry* (Thomas Nelson, 1936).

January 8, 1936 Hon. J.G. Gardiner, new Minister of Agriculture in the Federal house, and who won his byelection in Assiniboia day before yesterday, called the ministers of agriculture from the prairie provinces in Saskatoon today. The University, through its Agricultural faculty, was host to the guests at a dinner at the Bessborough Hotel tonight. I sat with Hon. Donald MacKenzie of Manitoba (originally North Brandon) and talked much about old times. In speaking, he referred to the days when Alex McEwan did their threshing and did it with a 44" separator, the biggest machine west of Winnipeg, and the gang which went with it was as big as the party assembled.

February 7, 1936 I talked at the Annual Agricultural Rally at Bounty. In spite of 40° F. below weather, there were 300 people present and many drove ten miles to be there. Topic of my talk—Romance of the Cattle Industry. The dance following the meeting lasted until 3 A.M.

I camped at Mr. & Mrs. Sam Adair's home, and had a good old fashioned visit around their kitchen stove. It was a sad day for our civilization when the kitchen stove was displaced by the furnace.

Mrs. Adair talks Gaelic, and gave me a little instruction. I feel the need of some Gaelic. If I can greet St. Peter in Gaelic, as he stands at the pearly gates, I'm sure I'll have no difficulty in getting by.

February 24, 1936 Mr. Melvin of Nelson's Publishing Co., Toronto, was our visitor today and tentative arrangements were made for the publishing of a text on Canadian Animal Husbandry by Al Ewen and myself.

March 4, 1936 The Saskatchewan Advanced Registry Swine Committee met at my office today and decided in favor of the continuation of the Feeding Station at the University.

Editor's Note: The University feeding station was partly funded by the federal government and enabled farmers to send their pigs to be fattened under controlled conditions. Close attention was paid to rate and economy of weight gain as well as the quality of the finished carcass.

March 24, 1936 The grand championship which came to rest today on the head of our University of Saskatchewan Galloway X Angus steer of 1934, brought to mind the deal we made with Lionel Stillborn one year ago. Stillborn, anxious to win the cup for the third time, came to the University one year ago and asked to buy one of our yearlings which he would carry over for show. We agreed to sell him a steer at .8¢ per lb., but no deposit was asked. After the balance of our cattle were marketed, Stillborn, having bought elsewhere, advised that he could not take the calf. We were left with the steer on our hands and as we were obliged to keep him, we fitted him and *we* won the cup for the third time.

April 10, 1936 (Good Friday) Knee deep in manuscript. We went to see the excellent picture, *Louis Pasteur*, this evening.

April 25, 1936 Attended a beef Cattle Meeting at Regina called by the Western Livestock Union to investigate the business. It was my proposal that some of the lower grades of beef now depressing the market might, to the profit of all, be placed in cans after proper processing. My observation that tough meat was usually well flavored and if the toughness could be overcome by correct processing (and it can be), a useful canned product might be put out. The packers present were skeptical, stating that they could not compete in that product with Argentina, yet retailers present complained that they were on occasion obliged to sell good shoulder roasts of beef at .5¢ per lb. I noticed in a Regina Safeway store that a 6 lb. tin of Argentina beef was offered as a special at 18¢ per lb. In small amounts it was 20¢ lb.

Grading of beef, either on foot or on the rail, was discussed. The majority favored rail grading of beef, although I found myself once again with the minority. Although recognizing the merit of carcass grading from a consumer's standpoint, I felt the time was not opportune for such. As yet only 8 to 10% of our beef is good enough for the two top grades now eligible for branding "Choice and Good." That means that the great bulk of our beef would be embarrassed by a low grade stamp such as medium, common or poor, and beef consumption might suffer.

May 14, 1936 Toronto. Nelson's accepted our book, "Science and Practice of Canadian Animal Husbandry."

I went up to Guelph this afternoon to complete some work on the manuscript and at the same time visit the MacEwans and see the old college. It was my good fortune to meet Prof. and Mrs. Jack Baker who drove me up around the O.A.C. where we inspected the Imported Clyde stallion "Craigie Realization," (Cawdor Cup 1933).

May 15, 1936 Toronto. Visited the Ontario Department of Agriculture where I secured some illustrations for the book. Did some "last minute" work on the text.

Heard a Highland drum and bugle band tonight. They were great. I followed them until I found myself over in West Toronto and miles from the station.

June 8, 1936 The joke on me this evening. When the electric toaster wouldn't work for me I took it apart and after an hour's work, when it was reassembled, I learned that the power had been off.

June 9, 1936 Drove to North Battleford for the cattle show and sale. It was a great failure. The high price of the sale was $75.00 and many bulls were unsold. We took 6 cows and heifers up and will bring 4 back.

June 28, 1936 Inducted Elder Knox Church by Dr. Jas. MacKenzie.

July 1, 1936 Phyllis and I drove to Aberdeen where we inspected several herds of pigs, including Clarence Gordon's and Geo. Huffman's.

July 2, 1936 Weyburn Fair for 4 hours. Between 1:30 P.M. and 4:30 P.M. I judged 49 classes of sheep. Took bus back to Regina.

July 11, 1936 Knee deep in galley proof of forthcoming book.

July 30, 1936 We began wheat cutting. The crop has deteriorated from a prospect of 40 bu. to 6 or 8 bu. per acre, owing to long hot spell without rain.

We purchased Maple (Colonial) furniture to extent of $276.50 from T. Eaton Co. today.

August 16, 1936 South of Tessier (12 miles) we visited the Thos. Wilson farm on which 6,200 acres of crop, including 4,000 acres of wheat, are being harvested. Wilson once used horses but is today on a tractor basis. Where once they had 200 horses, today they have a total of five. There are no cattle or pigs, although extensive barns indicate former endeavors at livestock raising. One barn cost $25,000 without labour.

September 5, 1936 A few days ago, 313 Bottomley Avenue was offered to us at what was against it—namely, $5,500.00. I offered $3,500 and they came down to $4,500.00. We inspected it yesterday and I offered $4,000. Today we got together at $4,250 cash. We negotiated with La Roche—MacDonald Agencies and the house built in 1931 was ostensibly the property of C.M. Suggitt.

September 9, 1936 Visited Jim MacKenzie's ranch where about 5,000 sheep are kept, and went on to Bell and Watt Martin's ranch where we will spend tonight.

It is a fine treat to see the Martin dogs, at the present time numbering 20 strong. Observations at the Martin's would tend to refute the theory that a working dog should not be petted. The dogs there are all treated as pals and even frequent the house. We saw Scotty, Meg and Flash who performed at Toronto Royal last fall. Mrs. Martin said, "Scotty has been our best dog, although Flash is Bill's favourite." The Martins are much isolated. Last winter they opened their Christmas mail on February 20. They are about 26 miles from Maple Creek.

October 25, 1936 Put in 2 cords Poplar wood seasoned at $6.50 per cord and 6 tons stove coal at $7.75 per ton.

December 18, 1936 I asked Phyllis what she wanted me to give her for Christmas and forthwith she presented me with a list of articles, with the names of the stores at which they could be purchased and the prices.

December 24, 1936 The MacEwan and Cline families are together at 313 Bottomley tonight. Mother and Dad MacEwan came in today.

December 25, 1936 The two families celebrated appropriately.

December 26, 1936 My father stands out as a splendid example of renewed youth. At the age of 66 he is having more fun and doing more to amuse and help his fellows than at any time in his life.

◆◆◆◆◆

IV
Professor to Politician
1937-1951

The following journal selections cover the final years at the University of Saskatchewan, and his removal to the University of Manitoba as Dean of Agriculture in 1946. The entries close with his defeat at the polls in the federal by-election for the City of Brandon in 1951. The two most pivotal events in MacEwan's life were his acceptance of the University of Manitoba position in 1946 and his political defeat five years later. Yet, these selections also contain some interesting glimpses into his life during these years. For instance, he travelled with historian A.S. Morton, seeking out relics of the fur trading era. The unsuccessful efforts to entice him into politics are also illuminative. Other important events during these years include the retirement and death of his parents, the birth of his daughter, Heather, and the purchase of land at Priddis, in the foothills near Calgary. He also gives a first-hand account of the Winnipeg flood of 1950.

The entries show his widening professional activities, and imply a growing restlessness. Unfortunately the entries become very brief towards the end and by the late 1940's, are mere chronicles. Yet, this too serves to underscore the fact that MacEwan's life was entering a new phase even before he left university work in 1951.

January 1937 My father recently returned from Winnipeg where he attended a meeting of the Western Canada Fairs Association. Writing on January 24, he stated, "It will take some time for me to get back to myself again. After engaging a room at the Fort Garry for $4.00 per night, I discovered there was no night there and as I am always in the habit of sleeping in the night, it was too much of a change for me."

February 25, 1937 The authors of "Science and Practise of Canadian Animal Husbandry" received their first royalty returns today. The statement shows 209 copies sold up to December 31, 1936, and each author received a cheque for $36.58 from Thos. Nelson and Sons, publishers.

March 1937 Jack MacPhail tells about that occasion when my father, as President of Melfort Agricultural Society, was negotiating for midway attractions or something of the kind. Anyway, the party retired to the hotel for some "refreshments." When it came time to go home, mother noticed that her man was not just right and said, "Alex, what's the matter with you?" His reply was, "There's not a thing wrong with me, but I've just had a drink out of a hell of a big bottle of whiskey."

March 25, 1937 It cost just $3.00 to learn from Dr. Generoux that I wasn't going to start wearing glasses for a while yet. My right eye is 100%; the left one could be a lot worse.

March 24, 1937 To fulfill an engagement with the Moose Jaw Milk Prod. Assn., I drove from Regina to Moose Jaw with Percy Reed and Al Ogilvie. There were more than 100 present at the noon meeting. Percy Reed read a fine tribute to the late J.A. Thompson, the grand old man of the dairy business. Carrying out Mr. Thompson's last instructions to me, I talked about the history of farming in the west and said "nothing about cows and dairying."

Editor's Note: MacEwan's companions were from the Saskatchewan Department of Agriculture. Reference to Thompson's last instructions concerns the latter's belief as stated in a conversation with MacEwan that governmental Depression remedies might well contribute to a welfare state mentality among farmers generally. Hence he wanted MacEwan to advance the notion through historical precedent of the role of individualism in building the rural west.

March 25, 1937 Sale of Shorthorn bulls at Regina. The sale was good with Chas. Sinclair's champion bringing $400.00. I bid on several of the good ones but failed to get one. The average price was $147.60 for 52 head and all bulls entered sold. The average was about $28.00 over that of last year. Our young bull brought $125.00.

Attended the annual meeting of the Sasaktchewan Aberdeen Angus Club. To Saskatoon tonight.

April 5, 1937 Prevailed upon by a good wife, I presented myself (not without objection) to medical inspection by Dr. David Baltzan. His judgement was "physically sound, except for minor throat infection, haemoglobin a bit low and evidence of fatigue." $3.00.

April 13, 1937 Phyllis MacEwan was the speaker at the final meeting of the Saskatoon Archaeological Society meeting for the year. Her topic was "The Inca culture."

April 19, 1937 G. MacEwan named Director of the new School of Agriculture which will replace the old associate course.

May 14, 1937 University convocation at which Premier Patterson gave the Address. I had the good fortune to be invited to Mr. and Mrs. Estey's home this evening to meet and talk with the Premier.

May 21, 1937 Along with some dignitaries, I was invited to inspect the first car of export pork products to go from Saskatoon. The car was made up mostly of hams, shoulders and backs from the (Pool Abattoir) Saskatchewan Co-op Live Stock Producers. The favored official guests were photographed.

June 1, 1937 Premier Stanley Baldwin retired from the head of the British Government and is succeeded by Premier Neville Chamberlain. It is told of Stanley Baldwin that the wish of his heart is "to retire to the country in Worcestershire, read the books he wants to read, live a decent life and keep pigs."

June 5, 1937 Phyllis and I were invited to Dr. and Mrs. Murray's dinner given for the outside staff of the University. I played the bagpipes.

Editor's Note: MacEwan is an enthusiastic fan of the pipes. In fact, in one of his rare requests for himself, he has requested that a pipe band play "Amazing Grace" at his funeral. Concerning his own ability with the pipes, MacEwan chuckles, shakes his head and admits he "wasn't very good."

June 7, 1937 My father, while loading a car of cattle for the Saskatoon spring show, broke and crushed his wrist and was taken immediately to the hospital. According to the story as told, he heard the bones collapsing and immediately called to Mother for the whiskey bottle. At the hospital, he was placed on the table, given chloroform and the bones set. While under the anaesthetic, the doctor, Dr. McKendry, pulled out the last nine teeth in the old gentleman's head.

Evidently, the doctor had been trying to persuade him to have these removed for a long time but he would never take time to have it done. Dad went home 24 hours after being admitted to hospital, nursing a big cast on his arm and toothless. Phyllis asks me if I'm a philosopher and quotes Socrates, "Marry by all means. If you get a good wife you will become very happy; if you get a bad one you will become a philosopher—and this is good for every man!"

June 17, 1937 Up at 5:30, Coles and I drive to Henry Chapman's at Belle Plaines, saw an excellent two year old (Gallinger bull) and a few good cows. From there back to Regina and to the Jail Farm where we inspected a recent shipment of 15 young boars from Ontario. The Percheron Stallion Rumulus looks splendid.

At the Jail Farm this morning, I acquired a pair of young orphan skunks, just walking. The mother was killed yesterday. The skunks arrived home with me this evening and although slow to take milk, after they had taken it, took a new and better lease on life. The sudden change from a creature of the wild to a devotee of man has occurred in eight hours.

June 18, 1937 Skunks doing well and already part of the household.

June 29, 1937 Saskatchewan crops pronounced the worst in history. Saskatchewan wheat estimated today at 90 millions or 6 bu per acre average, which is 2 bu per acre under the former low (1936). The situation over the entire province, with exception of a few small areas, is critical.

June 30, 1937 101°F in shade (official) with strong hot south wind; a

Grant with pet skunks, "This" and "That"

devastative day.

July 4, 1937 Phyllis and I took bus at 7 a.m. for Calgary. After two breakdowns and a lot of lost time, we arrived at our destination at 1 o'clock, an hour past midnight, to find all hotels filled. We located a poor bed in a private home.

July 6, 1937 We are thoroughly enjoying the Stampede and other things at Calgary.

July 8, 1937 After judging this evening, I visited John Burns and discussed biographical sketches of his late uncle, Pat Burns.

Editor's Note: This marked the beginnings of MacEwan's ongoing interest in Pat Burns which culminated in a biography over forty years later. While John Burns was very cooperative, MacEwan realized even then the paucity of written records pertaining to Burns' personal life.

July 9, 1937 Calgary to Saskatoon. The country for 300 of the 400 miles travelled looks desolate.

July 19, 1937 The skunks acquired on June 17 and descented on July 12, disappeared this morning. Their departure was a tragedy in the MacEwan home.

July 21, 1937 The skunks were found this morning in a deep toilet hole under the dressing room at the University Stadium. I managed to snare them with a piece of wire and draw them up. They spent most of today devouring food. After their arrival home, we disinfected them and reinstated the prodigals.

July 22, 1937 Judged Ayrshires at Saskatoon Exhibition. We began cutting Apex wheat on the University Farm. The crop is early and poor but miraculous, nevertheless, when one considers the absolute deficiency of moisture.

July 31, 1937 The crop on the University Farm can be fairly described as a failure. Most of our fields have already been pastured. We threshed the Apex wheat from No. 2 field this afternoon. There were 6 1/2 loads of sheaves from 53 acres and we got 84 bushels of wheat.

Misunderstanding produced peculiar results today. Phyllis' Mother left for her home today. Had she stayed, I was going to treat the family to dinner, but when she left I thought I was freed of the obligation. Phyllis thought that we two would have dinner downtown anyway and was waiting at Eatons from 12:45. In conversation with the dining room officials, she mentioned that it was a wedding anniversary dinner, following which advice the dietition said she would arrange a special table with flowers. The table was arranged and the decorations placed in order, but Phyllis' husband didn't come.

August 11, 1937 Phyllis got a fire screen ($12.94) for her birthday and I got a hunting butcher knife for mine.

August 26, 1937 My share of royalty on six months sales of "Science and Practise of Canadian Animal Husbandry" received today—$36.75. Total sales from September 1936 to June 30, 1937 were 420 copies.

August 28, 1937 The skunks have constipation. They have each had a dose of olive oil. We have between 65 and 70 loads of Russian thistles in the silo and ceased to ensile today. Can molasses was added to a part as a trial, the hope being to check putrifaction of the proteins by furnishing more available carbohydrates for bacterial attack. I expect to know a lot more about Russian thistles after this year. Phyllis and I tried Russian thistles for greens at dinner on August 22 and found the immature plants very much like spinach.

Editor's Note: MacEwan recalls that the only yield from the University's 1,000 crop acres was 200 loads of Russian thistles. The resulting experimentation with them as fodder was not overly successful. They were low on palatability and were intensely laxative. At their best they could be utilized as an emergency measure. Phyllis MacEwan remembers being somewhat appalled at being asked to experiment with them as salad as at that time they had not been tested on cattle. Certainly she was even less impressed at her husband's comment that one would never know if they were good for cattle without personal experimentation. Both admit that the thistles "were not very good to eat."

October 21, 1937 At my Father's sale today at which he was offering his herd of pure bred Aberdeen Angus cattle, he was asked if he would guarantee cattle purchased to stand up to the T.B. test. His public response was that he would and he added that if there was anything wrong with the cattle he was selling, he wanted to know it and would not allow a purchaser to take a loss. "Not only will I stand the loss on cattle that react to the bag test and more that that, I've got such faith in these cattle that I'll guarantee a living calf from every one of them." To the last remark, the hearers, having a sense of fairness and justice, protested and said, "No, you don't need to go that far, there'll be no guarantee of a living calf. The purchaser must take some of the risk."

Appearances are sometimes deceiving. At least, the neighbours who drove into the farmyard at Melfort just as my father was retreating at top speed across the yard and mother was following close behind, also at top speed, and swinging a broom as violently as possible, concluded a small family war. The truth was that Dad had decided to inspect his hive of bees and had neglected to properly clothe himself for the job. Anyway, a few bees got under his shirt and the balance of the swarm were considering attack when the old gentleman realized his predicament and took to his heels. At that moment, Mother came out of the house carrying her broom and when she saw my father's trouble, she became somewhat excited and in her determination to do something to help, took up the chase, frantically swiping at the few bees which were following my father.

Chas. Stewart of Pleasant Valley was the neighbour who drove into the yard and not seeing bees, seeing only a woman with a broom running after a poor fleeing man, considered that perhaps he came upon the scene at the wrong time.

October 30, 1937 Dr. J.S. Thomson, at the dinner for the School of Agriculture, said he didn't know much about farming but that he had learned to ride a mule, and for those who have never ridden a mule, "It's like being cast adrift in a rough sea in a small boat without a rudder."

November 13, 1937 Mother reminded Dad that a turkey would be required for the Presbyterian Church dinner. Dad was none too agreeable, but there were two turkeys in the band that had become a bit stiff and the others began picking on them. Dad expressed a wish that I would take a dressed turkey to Saskatoon. He disappeared and returned to tell Mother that the turkey was ready for the church dinner. He had killed two. "One is ready for the Presbyterians and I gave the other to the cats." The dressed birds were evidently disappointing.

November 20, 1937 Tragedy stalked the MacEwan house last night; the lad-skunk died after a sickness of four or five days. He had become quite a part of the family and while only a skunk, perhaps he could bring about as much credit and glory to his Creator as the average human of the present age. For aggressiveness, instinct, determination, olifactory capacity and understanding, he far excelled the female skunk which will be left to hibernate alone this winter. The best treatment we could think of failed to overcome the peculiar attack which he suffered. We buried him under the plum tree. Attachment is a funny thing.

November 23, 1937 While walking from Lestock to Touchwood on this date, I stopped to visit with an old Metis, born and reared in the country and of unknown age (probably 80 years or more). He lives with his daughter and three granddaughters, (no two of which are full sisters) and the five subsist on the old man's $15 pension. He lives a few yards from the old Fort Garry-Fort Edmonton Trail, still plainly in evidence. He was a man at Rebellion time and recalls his many buffalo hunting experiences of earlier years.

"You think you have many cattle; far more buffalo then than cattle now." He hunted both with gun and bow and arrow and had experience with the buffalo pound upon which he casts a new light.

According to his story, an oval-shaped pound, having a gate at each end and a tree in the centre, was constructed from poles. A rider went out to locate the herd and instead of driving the herd, he skirted it, himself secluded at the side of his horse and, while still under cover, he made a peculiar noise and struck off in the direction of the pound with the herd following. As he rode over a low pole (one foot above the ground) at the entrance of the corral, he slipped off his horse and remained below the pole which the oncoming buffalo leaped over. The horse continued to run through the corral and out at the opposite end, while two men with buffalo robes rushed out at the latter gate and turned the herd. The gates were stopped. The buffalo, contacting the tree, observed the tingle of the bell up in the tree and began to mill around the tree, usually going in one direction, fascinated by the bell. The slaughter began from several directions, continued until the last beast was down.

November 23, 1937 Doc Fawcett undertook to drive me to Touchwood that I might get the Transcontinental which stops at Touchwood to take on water. We drove on and sighted no elevators until past the Indian Residential School when we spotted the elevators. Doc F.'s daughter was operated on for appendicitis yesterday, so I volunteered to walk the remaining two miles to let him get on his way home to Regina. I walked on a mile and met an Indian on horseback. To make conversation, I asked him how far it was to Touchwood. He replied, it's 12 miles back to Touchwood by highway; you're just one mile from Lestock. There was but one thing to do, turn and wend a weary way back. I did. Between being lost in the bush when I attempted a short cut, visiting some Indians and breeds and arriving at Touchwood hungry, and finding neither store nor restaurant, it was an eventful day. From 8 a.m. until 10 p.m. I ate only an apple, a package of figs and a chocolate bar.

December 7, 1937 The School of Agriculture sponsored an amateur night which proved a good success. In Al Ewen's kilt, with George Hogg's pipes, I contributed a number to the programme.

December 16, 1937 At Saskatchewan Feed Board meeting at Regina at which the rations being allowed in relief areas were studied, and a recommendation made for some increases.

Editor's Note: This comment refers to the feed allowances instituted by the provincial government to alleviate some of the scarcities engendered by the Depression drought. Farmers received relief food for their livestock in this, according to MacEwan, the worst year of the Depression, 1937.

> *December 16, 1937* I spent an hour or so this evening with Z.M. Hamilton, old timer of Qu'Appelle country, now historian and writer living in Regina. He knew Pat Burns and other early notables. Mrs. Hamilton was a daughter of Pascal Bonneau, who went to Willow Bunch country and ranched from 1886. It was to Pascal Bonneau that Louis Riel's body was turned over after his death, and it was Pascal Bonneau's son who later accompanied the body to Winnipeg.
>
> I accompanied Mr. Hamilton to the CKCK studio where he delivered an address over CBC on Nicholas Flood Davin, Orator, Journalist and Statesman of early years in Canada and especially the West. He founded the *Regina Leader* in 1883.

Editor's Note: Hamilton was an amateur historian who had a particular interest in the Riel years. MacEwan had a high regard for this Scottish born historian and admits to being influenced by him in his own nascent historical career. Hamilton was a captivating storyteller and an excellent public speaker.

> *January 1, 1938* My resolve on this New Year Day, "to sing the church hymns for their meaning and to make the devotional part of church service count in 1938." Goodness knows, the minister's contributions are not proving what they should in changing troubled lives.

Editor's Note: Here is seen a significant indicator of MacEwan's declining interest in institutionalized religion.

> *March 12, 1938* MacEwan and Ewen sent a 400 page manuscript "General Agriculture" to Thos. Nelson and Sons, Toronto, today. It was written in less than four months.
>
> *May 9, 1938* His Excellency, Governor General Tweedsmuir, spent most of today at the University. He spent about 20 minutes to half an hour looking at our livestock. He was a most interested visitor. Although he looks half-starved and insignificant, he is a most delightful fellow to talk with and to walk about the barns with.
>
> *May, 1938* The surviving member of our famous pair of skunks burrowed under her pen during the night and is missing this morning.
>
> *May 20, 1938* Both the alley cat and Phyllis have spring fever. At 11:15 last night, the cat was on the roof of Thackeries' house and at 11:30, Phyllis was up there too, coaxing the cat to come down. Thackeries were in bed and their only protest was registered by the dropping of their window.
>
> *June 1, 1938* With O.S. Longman, Field Crops Commissioner for Alberta, I drove from Medicine Hat to High River, travelling via Vauxhall. We passed over the country at one time held by Canadian Land and Irrigation Co. with which J.D. MacGregor was associated. The irrigated land around Vauxhall was beautiful. Stopped for the night at High River.

Editor's Note: MacEwan speaks fondly of his trips with Arthur Silver Morton whom he refers to as "the Dean of Western Canadian historians." Morton was the expert and MacEwan the labouring apprentice. Morton, a noted authority on the fur trade, possessed an uncanny ability to ferret out the precise location of long-disappeared fur trading posts. He was, however, hopelessly impractical in the bush where, clad in a suit and hat, he would wander about oblivious to everything but his quest. MacEwan recalls that he "had the dickens of a time keeping track of the old man." Certainly it was Morton, more so than Hamilton, who provided the greatest single influence in the shaping of MacEwan the historian.

September 15, 1938   Professor Arthur Morton and I left early this morning to search for sites of old forts and trading posts in N.E. Saskatchewan. We began our search on the Upper Assiniboine, north of Canora, and made our night camp on the riverbank.

September 17, 1938   Efforts rewarded by the discovery of the sites of Carlton House (Hudson's Bay Co.) and Alexandria (N.W. Co.) on the south side of the Assiniboine on SW 33-32-3 W2. Only the small holes marking the old cellars, some below the bastions, remain. Carlton House was built in 1790 and abandoned about 1820.

This evening we journeyed N.E. to a small lake on the shore of which we searched for Peter Grant's trading house, but the exact location could not be discovered.

September 18, 1938   This morning we drove north from Pelly to the site of old Fort Livingstone, first capital of the Northwest Territories 1876-1877. "Here Lieutenant Governor Laird and His Council were sworn into office on 27th November, 1876, and here on 8th March, 1877, was held the first session of the North-West Council."

Our next jaunt was to look for Belleau's House on the east side of Snake Creek, about four miles west of Pelly. Unsuccessful.

To Old Fort Pelly, the Elbow of the Assiniboine and the Indian Reserve farther west. At the Reserve we were joined by Mr. Gilchrist (a Puchlinch man whose wife was a Galt Scot), and we searched the riverbank for a fort we did not find. Likewise, our search at the Elbow was fruitless, but we explored the site of Fort Pelly and also that of Old Fort Pelly from which location the post was moved on account of floods. Carlton House was superseded by Fort Hibernia and the latter by Fort Pelly. Fort Pelly was built about 1827.

September 19, 1938   We sketched the site of the old fort and drove on to look for Cuthbert Grant's house on the Assiniboine near Runnymede. We located the site on SW 1/4 14-28-31-1. I picked up a button probably worn by my namesake. Cuthbert Grant was father of the half-breed Cuthbert Grant who led the rebels in the massacre of Seven Oaks.

Inspected the "Thunder Bird" sketched on a large stone 1 1/2 miles east of Kamsack.

Stopped at Verigin on the return journey and chatted with Michael William Cazakoff, now secretary of the Doukhabor community. He was vice-president and general manager under Peter Verigin Sr. for 22 years, and has high regard for the old Peter. He was president four years after Peter Sr.'s death on November 29, 1924. He came with the first contingent of immigrants, arriving on Canada's sea coast late in 1898, and arriving on the site of the communtiy early in 1899. The first of them built shacks on section 27-29-1 south of Verigin, and also in the district of Arran. Peter Verigin came December 24, 1902 and remained at Verigan to 1924. Peter Verigin built his house in the village in 1910 and the big community store along side of it in 1920.

September 29, 1938 A European war, which yesterday seemed inevitable, today appears to be averted as a result of a conference of premiers of four nations: Chamberlain of Britain, Mussolini of Italy, Hitler of Germany and Daladier of France.

October 19, 1938 On air in connection with Cockshutt programme with topic, "Wheat as a Feed." 4 1/2 minutes.

October 22, 1938 This is Dad's birthday. I asked him how old he is. He paused in thought and said, "Blamed if I'm sure, but it's 69 or 79." I think it is 69.

December 6, 1938 C.B.C. "How Horses Came to Western Canada." (Cheque for $20.00 on April 27, 1939).

Editor's Note: These periodic radio talks on CBC were the forerunners of the "Sodbuster" series which in turn marked the beginnings of MacEwan's historical writings.

December 12, 1938 Winnipeg for Premier Bracken's conference on Agricultural Markets.

January 20, 1939 I acted on the Examining Committee for a civil service position at the Melfort Exp. Station.

January 21, 1939 Perhaps it is just coincidence but at Regina today, the three members of the examining board (civil service job) were MacLeod, McPhail and MacEwan. The three candidates who were to be examined were all Englishmen and all failed.

January 25, 1939 At the Livestock Breeders Convention banquet tonight, the roll of honour was presented by my father. The Livestock Board, a few years ago, initiated the practise of conferring such an honour on one breeder each year. Mother and Dad came down yesterday, had a picture taken and are having the time of their lives. The sire responded to the presentation of the scroll tonight and got the biggest applause of the programme. He won the title of the "Will Rogers" of Western Canada.

Editor's Note: MacEwan remembers this speech well. Apparently, MacEwan Sr. began nervously and was clearly ill at ease. Then at the whispered bidding of a close friend at the head table, the chairs were all pushed close to the table giving the old man room to parade up and down. This did the trick, and Alex MacEwan waxed eloquent all the time striding up and down with typical MacEwan vigour.

February 23, 1939 With Claude Gallinger, drove to his farm at Tofield and inspected one of Canada's premier herds of Shorthorns.

March 3, 1939 Spoke to Rosetown Board of Trade on "Trends in Prairie Agriculture."

May 3, 1939 Phyllis to hospital at 11 a.m. HEATHER MacEWAN born at 11:45 p.m. Length 23", head 14 1/2", hair black and lots of it. Disposition good. Proof that a good sire pays.

May 27, 1939 Following the Fat Stock Show of the past two days at which my sire did especially well both in prizes and prices, I suggested to him that he should "blow" himself to something. In other words, give himself a real treat. He replied, "Believe I will, think I'll buy a new porridge pot." He did and was thrilled with the acquisition.

August 11, 1939 Heather christened at Forestry Farm by Dr. John Nicol.

September 2, 1939 Britain and France have declared war on Germany and the nations go forward to another World War.

September 3, 1939 "General Agriculture" by MacEwan and Ewen off the press. A. Thomas Nelson & Sons Book, it will retail at $1.50.

February 1940 Uncle John Grant's comment when he saw my picture in one of the papers was that "I looked like a man who lived a temperate life and kept the Sabbath."

Dr. Vic Graham gave me a bottle of yeast culture to use in connection with a chokecherry wine experiment. Walking home this evening, in company with Nan McKay, the bottle in my hip pocket was naughty. The lid blew out with a notorious "pop" and I was too much embarrassed to explain to my company that it was a cork.

September 4, 1940 On way home tonight I had humiliating experience of finding myself in a pullman car alley, naked and unable to find my berth. I had been walking in my sleep, and how I got out of my upper berth without unbuttoning the curtains, will never be known.

December 22, 1940 Phyllis reminds me that I'm "short of shirts." I have five that I know of and I immediately think back to the time when I had only one shirt and two pairs of soxs and was never stuck. She is not ready to agree that such experiences of youthful days are something warranting thanksgiving. Her own youth was much different from mine. While I struggled as a poor but hopeful youngster, she was the proud owner of a fur coat and a team of Shetland ponies, and was able to winter in California. Somehow, I feel convinced that the child that does not have too many luxuries and who is required to struggle a bit, has a great advantage later on, has a finer sense of values and a different form of sympathy. Perhaps I'm wrong, but I must be shown.

December 25, 1940 Out to a Christmas party last night and one h--- of a party it was. It was one of those parties at which everything possible is done to increase a sane person's displeasure. In the first place, Christmas Eve is a time when one should be at home. But to reward evil for good, after I had done them the courtesy of accepting an invitation I didn't want, they asked that dress suits be worn. And that was not all; what might have been good food and pure was spiced to the point where it was unrecognizable, unpalatable, unchristian and indigestible; the house was hot and sleepy, the guests refused determinedly to discuss anything of an intelligent nature and I was obliged to pay honest money for taxi service both going and coming. Why do men do these things? However, I take some satisfaction from the fact that I was not more than half hypocrite; I thanked the hostess but my conscience wouldn't let me say that it was an enjoyable evening.

January 4, 1941 Calgary today. At 9 a.m. went out to look at piece of land on Fish Creek owned by F.G. Lenn Renfrew Motors, 326 - 5 Avenue W., Calgary and at 11 o'clock a deal was made by which I bought the half of 23-22-3 W5 $12 per acre.

Editors' Note: This piece of property at Priddis is still in the family. Heather MacEwan Foran and family have resided there since 1974. MacEwan himself did a lot of clearing on the property and has been a regular visitor to the log cabin built by his Uncle John in the 1940's. Incidentally, Phyllis MacEwan was not overly impressed at the time with this purchase, believing that the MacEwan money might be put to better use in the still lean economic times. She has long since changed her mind and Priddis remains her favorite spot.

January 22, 1941 At the Livestock Breeders' Convention at Regina this evening, the unpredictable Archibald MacNabb, Lieutenant Governor of Saskatchewan was to be guest of honour at the annual banquet in the Hotel Saskatchewan. At 6:15, the hour set for the banquet to commence, 600 people stood in the approach to the banquet hall waiting for the King's representative to arrive and take his place. Fifteen minutes passed and the governor's party had not arrived; 30 minutes passed and still no sign of Honourable A.P. MacNabb. Forty minutes after the time set for the banquet to commence, ''Archie,'' wearing the characterisitc grin, arrived and 600 weary and hungry people filed about the tables. My place was at the head table, next to Miss Ruby McConnell, the secretary at Government House and I ventured a question about the reason for Mr. MacNabb's late arrival, hoping that there had been no car trouble or sickness. A little reticent, the Lieutenant Governor's secretary disclosed that ''His Honour was involved in a rummy game and was winning. He won $1.40.''

March, 1941 Mother, in her letter of March 13, 1941, wrote, ''Dad is still getting up at 4 a.m. and he goes steadily all day. This morning he lit the fire as usual, but there was a high wind and he heard a loud noise and discovered that the chimney was on fire. When our chimney burns, it is no ordinary fire; the flames were reaching the sky. He didn't wake us up, but got a ladder and a pail and climbed onto the roof. Clarence (hired man) awoke with this awful noise above his head and thought the Germans were here. He got up as quickly as he could and found Dad sitting on top of the house with his pail, ready to shovel snow if the roof took fire. That was long before daybreak.''

April 24, 1941   I sent the manuscript for ''The Breeds of Farm Live Stock in Canada'' to Nelsons, Toronto, today. It now appears that some money from the ''Horned Cattle Fund,'' Saskatchewan Department of Agriculture, will be advanced to ensure that the new book will get a start.

April 26, 1941   Calgary and Priddis. T.O. Renner will pasture his cattle and horses on west half of 23-22-3-5 at 50 cents per month for cattle and 75 cents for horses. Hugh McNair, R.R. No. 1, Midnapore, will summer-fallow and seed grass on cultivated land and collect $2 per acre.

Editors' Note: The Renner family continues to pasture cattle there, making the association over forty years old.

June 25, 1941   103.7° official at Saskatoon with strong hot wind. Judged light horses at Moose Jaw and was tossed from horse in first class, landing on a brittle collar bone.

June 28, 1941   Took possession of new Plymouth coach, $1,327.59 plus insurance; $37.00.

June 29, 1941   To Brandon Fair with Mr. W.I. Munroe, Jack Warren and Sid Johns, in former's private car, C.N.R.

July 11, 1941   Under the auspices of the Western Stock Growers Ass'n., a beef cutting demonstration was held in the Victoria Pavilion at Calgary Exhibition and I was asked to take it. About 300 or 400 people witnessed it.

August 1, 1941   Percy Reed kindly offered to drive Dean Kirk and me downtown from the Regina Fair. We were late for an appointment. As the car sped away from its parking place, there was a roar, a tear and crash. Percy stopped quickly to discover that the bumper of his car had become caught in a tent rope of the big Beatty Washer tent at the fairgrounds. The tent was flat on the ground; the poles were all down; the canvas was torn and the equipment spread over the ground. And from underneath there emerged a surprised and worried man.

September 12 & 13, 1941   Exploring with Dr. A.S. Morton in northeastern Saskatchewan, along the Assiniboine mostly. A successful trip and a number of old fort sites were located.

September 16, 1941   To Melfort to see MacEwans. Heather's first trip to Melfort. MacEwans announce the sale of all their farm equipment on September 25, 1941.

Editor's Note: MacEwan had encouraged his parents to give up farming. Bertha was in poor heatlh and Alex was finding the winters increasingly difficult. Following the disposal of their farm and animals, the MacEwans moved to White Rock, British Columbia.

September 25, 1941   Dad's sale at Melfort. The pure bred cattle were sold primarily, and the horses he refused to sell, the latter must be destroyed humanely or remain on the farm where they have worked. The auction sale began at 12 noon and car lights were used on the last articles to be sold at 7 o'clock.

MacEwan on camping trip with A.S. Morton on Assiniboine River.

Dad announced tonight that Jack Gammie, good neighbour to the north, would rent the farm for three years. Jack will live on the MacEwan farm and work his own place from there.

October 25, 1941 To Fort La Corne and intermediate points with Dr. Morton on jaunt for purpose of locating fort sites. We found the site of the post on Mosquito Point after navigating the Saskatchewan River northeast of Weldon in a boat of doubtful dependability. Dr. Morton related that we were more nearly drowned in the boat than we were in the river.

November 21, 1941 Calgary—collected $37 plus $6 pasture rent for Priddis half from T.O. Renner.

With J.C. Leslie, drove south to look at two-section place owned by Burns and Co., just south of mine.

December 2, 1941 Things developed rapidly last night and this afternoon I took plane for Chicago to attend a meeting called by A.W. Peterson of Ottawa and simultaneously attend International Fat Stock Show.

April 15, 1942 Ottawa is a mad-house. Here for agriculture supply meetings, mainly about increasing sheep and wool production.

August 8, 1942 Phyllis and I in Calgary. Went this morning to High River and then west to Longview with Mr. Frank Watt to look at piece of land. Attracted by land which has abundance of grass and is watered by Highwood River.

August 15, 1942 Left with Prof. Morton to inspect old fort sites north. Spent this evening at Duck Lake and looked over the N.W. Rebellion battleground west of Duck Lake. Brocklebank, Craig Miller, Dean Munroe and Furniss are with us.

Editor's Note: MacEwan's and Morton's companions in the party were members of the Saskatchewan Historical Society. Morton apparently was cultivating their interest, hoping that the society might support him in his quest to have selected historic sites fenced and maintained.

August 16, 1942   To Fort Carlton and along with North Saskatchewan River to Prince Albert.

September 1, 1942   Harvest season very late and that, combined with labour shortage and heavy crop, makes the season a worrisome one.

September 7, 1942   Labour Day. Saskatoon Riding Club Horse Show, fine success. MacEwan won a show halter offered by M. Grummet for first in the bareback wrestling event.

December 16, 1942   I was elected president of the Saskatoon Exhibition Association.

December 29, 1942   CBC (western) with first of a four talk series, "Sodbuster Series." Tonight it was "Captain John Palliser, Sodbuster No. 1."

February 1, 1943   I was pallbearer at funeral of "Unknown Sodbuster," Wm. E. McClelland who died January 28.

Editor's Note: W.E. McClelland was born in Red Deer, Alberta and was a noted horse pioneer. He gave MacEwan his story but kept his identity anonymous on the insistence of his wife.

February 5, 1943   I go to Edmonton tonight to review proposed position of Director of Animal Production for province.

April 19, 1943   Regina for meeting of Western Canada Fairs Association representatives to discuss transportation problems. Met Mr. Jas. Gardiner. Sid Johns and I were named to carry the problem to the east and interview Mr. T. Lockwood, Transport Controller of Canada.

April 28, 1943   Meeting in Montreal with Mr. T. Lockwood, Transport Controller. Ruling is "no special trains for fairs, but free use of regular freights."

July 8, 1943   Pleasant and interesting visit with Sally Rand and Turk Greenough of Red Rock, Montana.

Editor's Note: Sally Rand was a well-known fan dancer and entertainer. She, and her husband Turk Greenough, owned a ranch in Montana. Sally Rand had invited MacEwan to visit and proffer advice on ranch and livestock management. When teased by family and friends on his friendship with a glamorous fan dancer, MacEwan habitually replies with a straight face that "she had a good mind."

July 20, 1943   Saskatoon Exhibition opens. Old Timer's Day at Fair, and the Barr Colonists who arrived here 40 years ago are special guests of honour.

July 24, 1943   A second livestock parade this Saturday morning. The first was on Thursday night. The one this morning was a fine success with about 3,500 boys and girls out. Mr. Fred Mendel gave a pony away and then when the lucky boy was found to be from Pennant instead of Saskatoon, Fred Mendel gave another one.

Tonight we look back upon one of the most successful shows in Saskatoon's history.

August 9, 1943   I was honoured with the responsibility of officially opening North Battleford fair. Judged some cattle too.

October 10, 1943   Arrived Ashcroft, British Columbia late at night and went to hotel. Got last room available and announced my intentions of catching early morning bus north. Said, ''Please call me at 7:30.'' The response from the keeper was a bit startling. ''I'll call you at 7:00; I call everybody at that hour.''

Editor's Note: MacEwan regularly visited this area of British Columbia for judging purposes. Indeed, his ongoing judging commitments enabled him to further his knowledge of western Canadian communities.

October 11, 1943 Bus north from Ashcroft over Cariboo Trail to Williams Lake. The old trail vibrates with romance, and one has a feeling that the old stopping houses and the snakey trail are trying to tell their secrets about pack trains, hold-ups, gold, tragedy, etc. It is beautiful as well as romantic.

Ashcroft, by the way, is the driest point in B.C., precipitation 6.3''.

October 13, 1943 2,500 commercial cattle out, although not all in the show. Every one of those 2,500 walked over the trails to Williams Lake. Some came over 200 miles, the trail journey taking 23 days. Those coming the greatest distance were from the vast Chilcotin country to the west. The cattle are good, showing lots of quality. They are all Herefords. The people are exceptionally kind and appreciative. Enjoyed the judging.

October 14, 1943 Sale of cattle at Williams Lake. Mat Hassen selling. After the sale I was driven by Lord Martin Cecil, of 100 Mile House, to the Foreward Ranch for a visit with Mrs. Cowan, Proprietor.

Banquet tonight and me the speaker.

Big event of today, Klondyke Night. It is an all-out effort and lasts until 4 or 5 a.m. Indians, cowboys and even those who consider themselves superior, go and dance and drink and gamble.

October 15, 1943 Judged the Williams Lake bull show, prior to the bull sale. Immediately after the show, I went south with Doc Carlyle, our first stop being Alkali Lake Ranch where we were royally received by the prosperous and gracious proprietor, Mr. Reideman. He is Austrian and evidently of noble birth. He has the most attractive ranch and grass range I've seen in the interior.

Our next stop was farther south where one looks westward over a gigantic expanse of rough country extending to the coastal range; the Cascades. The Gang Ranch, on the opposite side of the Fraser, is seen, or at least a part of it. The Gang is the biggest ranch in the Chilcotin and the cattle can roam over a range of some 2,400 square miles, bounded on the east by the Fraser; Churn Creek on the south, Big Creek on the west and 30 miles of Chilcotin River on the north. When the 22 Gang rides set out to do the June round-up, they have a 10 day job on their hands, and probably they never find them all.

November 8, 1943 Offered position of Secretary-Manager of Exhibition at Saskatoon.

Editor's Note: MacEwan accepted the position which he held for two years.

November 21, 1943 Dined this evening with Hon. J.G. Gardiner who has asked me to go into politics, and suggests Saskatoon City for next Federal.

Editor's Note: Several entries following refer to efforts by the federal Liberals, provincial Liberals and provincial Conservatives to entice MacEwan into the political arena. He had a good following in rural areas, and was therefore considered a prime political prospect. Not being a Conservative he turned John Bracken down even though it was suggested that the Conservative label be removed thorugh the formation of a new party, the Saskatchewan Agrarian Party. As for the provincial Liberals, MacEwan was of the opinion that the party was destined for defeat and that his candidacy would be of little consequence. He rejected Jimmy Gardiner's federal overture because he felt he was not ready. He reflects that though ostensibly a Liberal at the time, he was not a strong party man which may help explain why he listened to Bracken's Conservative offer.

January 18, 1944 Visit from Dick Bell, organizer for Progressive Conservative party.

January 19, 1944 Spent forenoon in Regina with John Bracken. The proposal is that I lead the Progressive Conservative party in Saskatchewan.

March 1, 1944 Phyllis' father died this morning.

Editor's Note: Vernon Cline was a station agent with the C.P.R. An active, clean-living family man, his sudden death at age 59 was a terrible shock to the family. His widow, Ethel, lived intermittently with her daughters Phyllis and Gertrude until shortly before her death.

March 4, 1944 Mr. Cline's funeral at Saskatoon.

March 13, 1944 To Regina tonight at behest of Mr. Patterson. Same questions, "Will you consider going into politics?"

April 9, 1944 Session with Premier Patterson, Regina. Wants me to go into provincial politics.

April 13, 1944 Met Uncle John Grant in Calgary and drove out to Priddis. We walked over the place and selected site for cabin with lots of scenery.

Editor's Note: The cabin was built by John, assisted by an Indian from the nearby Sarcee Reserve. It still stands, being used by the family for social occasions. Its location commands a panoramic view of foothills and mountains.

May 1, 1944 Winnipeg, en route to Ottawa for P.F.F.A. meetings.

Editor's Note: P.F.A.A. refers to the Prairie Farm Assistance Act. MacEwan was on the Board of Review, being an appointee of Jimmy Gardiner, Minister of Agriculture. The Act assisted farmers whose crops had failed.

June 6, 1944 Calgary. Hitch-hiked to Priddis, found John Grant completing chinking of log house.

July 5, 1944 Warman Field Day and won a ton of coal for guessing production on a Holstein cow.

July 18, 1944 I was to speak to Kiwanis on "The Story of the Fairs." I received a nice introduction from Chairman Emment Hall and as I rose to speak, everybody in the hall got up to leave. The speaker was speechless, but when the joke was apparent, they all returned to their seats and to fairly decent behaviour.

July 17, 1944 Story reached me from Calgary today. Jock Falkoner of Melfort was judging Clydesdales at Calgary last week. Thursday, when he was working in the show ring, a telegram was handed to him reporting that his wife had died. There was consternation about the ring and Charles Yule expressed sorrow and told Jock he need not do any more judging, Charlie would find someone to finish. But Jock said, "That's all right. I'll finish the judging; I made all the arrangements for the funeral before I left home." Jock finished judging.

July 25, 1944 Old Timer's Day at Exhibition. Rained heavily while Indian Pageant in progress in evening. Mr. Eby and I, who were judging costumes, got soaked. The old gent said, "MacEwan, I forded the Saskatchewan River a couple of times first year in the country, but I never got as wet as this." Chief Harry Littlecrow was "advising" us about the winner and after the names were announced in each class, it was clear that Harry had recommended the members of his own family.

August 19, 1944 With Brock and Morton and others to South Branch House (St. Louis) to erect fence around historic site.

August 25, 1944 During night, somebody removed a wheel and tire from my car and left it sitting on a block.

September 1, 1944 Tore finger getting over fence and away from Holstein bull.

September 6, 1944 Regina for meeting called to discuss markets for surplus horses.

October 31, 1944 Chairman of Kiwanis luncheon. Elected vice-president for first quarter of 1945.

November 29, 30/44 Toronto attending meetings of Canadian Association of Exhibitions. Made vice-president.

December 12, 1944 Annual meeting of Saskatoon Exhibition Board. Gave my retiring president's report. Reported $27,000 net profit for past year.

December 26, 1944 Wire from Dad advising Mother passed away last night. Will leave with body on tomorrow night eight fifty for Melfort. "YOU ARRANGE WITH MELFORT UNDERTAKER TO MEET TRAIN AND PREPARE GRAVE. DAD."

December 29, 1944 Dad arrived here at Saskatoon and he and I went on at noon to Melfort for the funeral tomorrow. Mother was not sick for long. She had been up Christmas morning and opened her parcels, but in afternoon went to bed. Dad called doctor at 4 p.m. but he did not arrive until after 10. Mother passed on just before midnight Christmas Day. Dad reported that she was perfectly at ease and slipped into the next world without pain and breathing freely. Just slept peacefully away but the doctor remained, knowing that she was going.

December 30, 1944 Mother's funeral very lovely. The little St. James Church was full of old friends in spite of severe cold. The many floral tributes beautiful and Mother's face was beautiful. The Pallbearers were Rod

McLeod, Doc Dunbar, Jack McPhail, Jack Gammie, Chester Magnuson and Robert Hastie. The minister was Prof. H. Dubois and the hymns were: (1) Unto the Hills Do I Lift Up My Longing Eyes; (2) Rock of Ages; (3) Awake My Soul; O Love That Wilt Not Let Me Go.

Mother's body was placed beside the grave of her youngest boy at Mount Pleasant Cemetery.

January 11, 1945 Announced from Montreal that I was today made a director of Royal Bank of Canada.

January 29, 1945 Pallbearer at funeral of late Prof. A.S. Morton, grand old historian.

February 9, 10, 1945 Attending Advisory Committee on beef cattle, Toronto.

March 23, 1945 Dr. W.C. Murray died this morning.

March 26, 1945 Returned to Saskatoon for Dr. Murray's funeral, pallbearer.

Editor's Note: MacEwan held Walter Murray, President of the University of Saskatchewan, in the highest esteem. He offers this contemporary comment: "As I think back, I consider knowing Dr. Murray my greatest University experience. I knew him as a capable administrator, the greatest of company and one of God's finest gentlemen."

May 20, 1945 Grant MacEwan gave the sermon at Westminster Church for Rev. Art Moore who is at Moose Jaw. Theme, "Good Will, A Prairie Tradition."

September 4, 1945 Heather MacEwan started to school. After first half day she was home early, and phoned her Daddy to report progress. Dad said, "Did you learn anything at school?" and the reply was, "Yes, Daddy, I learned where the toilets are."

September 16, 1945 Saw Priddis and Longview and had a good drink from the spring.

Spetember 17, 1945 Offered position of Manager of New Canadian Council of Beef Producers.

September 22, 1945. Home. First of galley proofs of new book, "Feeding Live Stock," arrived.

October 26, 1945 Meeting of Murray Memorial Committee at which Grant MacEwan was asked to manage campaign.

Editor's Note: The Murray Memorial Committee had, as its goal, the Walter Murray Library at the University. While this facility was eventually built, it was not a direct product of this committee which, however, did raise close to $100,000.

October 30, 1945 T.C.A. (Trans Canada Airlines) Regina to Toronto to see sick Dad.

October 31, 1945 Dad very sick man. I arrived at hospital at 1:30 a.m. and remained with him all night. But at 4:30 a.m. his nurse recognizing my sleepiness, suggested I crawl under the sheet on a vacant bed. I did and slept soundly, until the new shift of nurses came on. Then I was awakened by a nurse and a thermometer was shoved into my mouth.

Editor's Note: Alexander MacEwan had originally gone to Guelph to visit his sister when he became ill and was admitted to hospital in Toronto. He remained there until his death in November.

November 14, 1945 My father passed on to his rest today. He would be 76 at his next birthday. He was a good and sensible father. The body will be brought to Melfort for burial.

November 18, 1945 Dad's funeral at Melfort. The little church (St. James) was full and Mr. Bell conducted the service. The pallbearers and the hymns were the same as for Mother's funeral service, from the same church 10 months ago. Uncle Jim and John Grant, patriarchs, were up from Brandon for the funeral. It does one good to see them.

Uncles Jim and John Grant are two wonders and two of life's best sermons. They learned to live.

One of Jim's sage remarks came when we were driving through Melfort; he observed that Melfort was a clean town, no slum district like they have in Brandon.

December 11, 1945 Meeting marking official opening of Murray Memorial Fund. His Honour, the Lt. Governor, was chairman and Hon. Woodrow Lloyd, main speaker. Grant MacEwan is chairman of Murray Memorial Committee.

Editor's Note: From this point the diary entries become very brief and mostly a chronicle of events. The two significant events in MacEwan's life in these years, 1946-51, were his acceptance of the Deanship of Agriculture at the University of Manitoba, August 1946, and his bid for a federal seat in Brandon in 1951.

January 8, 1946 Installation of Kiwanis officers for 1946, Grant MacEwan, President.

May 22, 1946 Heather got a pony, $75; bought her from Lundy's. The name is to be Molasses.

July 8, 1946 Annual meeting of Canadian Palomino Association, Grant MacEwan, new President, at Calgary.

August 21, 1946 President Trueman of University of Manitoba and Mr. Parker of Board of Governors offered me Deanship for Agriculture. I accepted.

August 22, 1946 Home to Saskatoon. Appointment at Manitoba confirmed. On C.B.C. tonight, "The Man Murray."

August 25, 1946 Back to Winnipeg with Phyllis and bought Ross Cavers' house at 814 Somerset Avenue, $7,000 cash.

September 3, 1946 I requested grant for Murray Memorial from city council and got $2,000.

September 4, 1946 Sold house at 313 Bottomley Avenue to Mrs. Lillian A. Smith for $8,500 cash.

September 5, 1946 On C.B.C., "Clement Cornwall, Ashcroft Pioneer." Exhibition Board dinner at which Grant MacEwan was presented with a china horse, a replica of the real horse to be given to me next week.

September 10, 1946   Grant MacEwan Day at Kiwanis Club. This afternoon I was formally presented with the Exhibition Board's gift horse, a two year old Palomino gelding.

September 14, 1946   Saskatoon Riding Club party for MacEwans. Received framed picture and tooled bridle.

September 16, 1946   University of Saskatchewan faculty party. Grant MacEwan given a pen and pencil set, Waterman.

September 17, 1946   Loaded everything in McCosham van and left Saskatoon by car.

September 27, 1946   Manitoba Agriculture grads banquet to welcome Grant MacEwan; lovely affair.

October 1, 1946   My first faculty council meeting.

June 10, 1947   Heather to hospital for operation for tonsils.

June 11, 1947   Heather operated on this morning, OK.

July 7-11, 1947   Calgary, judged Clydes, Thoroughbreds and did parade.

July 22-25, 1947   At Saskatoon Exhibition. Judged Shorthorns and Angus and did commentary on parade.

July 22, 1947   Heather playing with Ruth Peborty, broke her arm.

July 12, 1948   At Edmonton—to Leduc oil fields to see wild Atlantic No. 3, spouting 10,000 barrels of oil over several acres per day.

August 20, 1948   New book, "The Sodbusters" arrived.

Editor's Note: This represents the first of MacEwan's historical publications.

November 8, 1948   Inauguration of President Gillson.

November 11, 1948   Doug Campbell, Premier Elect, wants me to join Manitoba government in agriculture.

November 24, 1948   Decided against politics in Manitoba government.

Editor's Note: MacEwan recalls that at the time he was not particularly interested in anchoring himself in Manitoba. The idea of residence in Alberta was already a germ in the back of his mind. Hence his rejection of Campbell's offer.

November 25, 1948   Manitoba Union of Municipalities, "Science in our Time."

March 1, 1949   University convocation at which Mrs. Eleanor Roosevelt was given honorary degree.

March 21, 1949   Made deal with Dr. Pierce to publish horse story.

Editor's Note: Pierce was a director of Ryerson Press. The deal was a verbal agreement to publish a book on horses. Though MacEwan wrote a manuscript it was never published. However, it finally appeared in book form revised and rewritten many years later under the title of *"Hoofprints and Hitching Posts"* (1964).

June 22, 1949   Pepita foaled. Filly foal. Wired Heather, "Pepita has baby girl, beautiful blonde, naming her Sally."

August 7, 1949   Flew to Los Angeles.

Editor's Note: Apparently, at the time, there was no sustained breeding pro-

gramme of Arabians in Saskatchewan. MacEwan was asked to go to California
to view some leading Arabian establishments with a view to a possible publication heightening local interest in Arabians.

August 8, 9, 10   Touring southern California Arabian studs.

October 7, 1949   Freshman Day Parade. Heather and I rode in Home
Economics section, Heather on her recently acquired Daisy Mae mare.

January 16, 1950   Western Association of Exhibitions, proposal to write
history of fairs and exhibitions.

Editor's Note: The following entries document some of MacEwan's experiences
in the flood of 1950. It was not the highest flood that Winnipeg had or would
see. The years 1826, 1852 and 1961 were higher. Still, it was formidable enough.
Some 75,000 people were evacuated, including Phyllis and Heather MacEwan.
At night, MacEwan manned the graveyard shift on the sewer gang in an effort
to keep the sewers open. During the day, his time was spent mainly in trying
to feed the university livestock from a rowboat. Following the flood, he was
a member of the three man Red River Valley Board which administered over
$35 million in rehabilitation funds from the two levels of government.

May 1, 1950   Red River rising ominously.

May 7, 1950   Floods threatening.

May 8, 1950   Took university offices at Broadway because Pembina
Highway cut.

May 12, 1950   Evacuated family to Saskatoon. Floods increasingly serious.

May 13, 1950   Water 30.1'' above.

May 15, 1950   To university by boat from Municipal Hall and had misfortune to get in with two half-drunken boatmen. Collided with other boat. Some
cattle being evacuated to Brandon, hauled out behind a tractor. Other cattle
quartered in freight cars on university; pigs in cars and sheep in loft.

All Winnipeg meetings cancelled owing to flood.

May 24, 1950   I'm on "sewer gang," 3 a.m. and 6 a.m.

May 29, 1950   Premier Campbell appointed me to Red River Valley Board,
for rehabilitation purposes. Promises to be big and perhaps long.

May 30, 1950   Helicopter trip over the valley. My first.

June 4, 1950   With Joslyn, Col. Baldwin, Mayor Harry Shewman, to Morris
to see the worst devastation of all. Last part of journey by boat. Morris with
1200 population, 368 homes and 51 businesses placed. All homes except
four had water over floors and 41 homes floated away or collapsed. It is
a sickening and sour mess.

January 26, 1951   MacEwan party for faculty in the new home ec building.
Hon. James Gardiner danced the Sailor's Hornpipe.

March 17, 1951   Visited Brandon quietly to receive Liberal invitation for
federal by-election.

Editor's Note: The invitation was extended by the executive of the Brandon
Liberal Association. MacEwan admits today that he was uncertain over the whole
thing, and mentions that Louis St. Laurent, Prime Minister of Canada, had hinted

at a cabinet post. This challenge, plus his growing disenchantment with university work, led him to contest a seat that presumably was his for the taking.

April 19, 1951 Nomination Day, Brandon constituency.

May 19, 1951 Faculty of Agriculture-Home Economics party for MacEwans.

Editor's Note: In order to contest the federal seat, MacEwan had to resign from his university position. This was the farewell party given to him.

June 25, 1951 By-election, Brandon—defeated by Dinsdale.

Editor's Note: MacEwan cites several reasons for his defeat including current unpopular Liberal grain policies and the penchant for government candidates to be defeated in by-elections. Possibly the most pivotal factor, however was the popularity and support enjoyed by his opponent. A well-known local educator, Walter Dinsdale campaigned actively on his name and reputation.

MacEwan carried on his journals to the end of 1951. The entries however are too sparse to be of any real interest. Following his defeat at the polls, he worked for a time as agricultural editor of the *Western Producer* before accepting a position as General Manager of the Canadian Council of Beef Producers (Western Section). It was in this latter capacity that he moved his family to Calgary in the summer of 1952. During the period 1952-58, he continued to write and became actively involved in politics at the municipal and provincial levels. He did not keep a journal during this time or thereafter for that matter, except for brief periods in 1958-59 and 1963-65.

◆◆◆◆◆

V
A Leader's Devotion
1958-1965

This final selection of journal entries covers two separate periods. The first from November, 1958 to June, 1959, details MacEwan's activities as leader of the Alberta Liberal Party in the election campaign of 1959. The journal shows his hectic travelling schedule, his assessment of candidates for election, as well as some light-hearted barbs at the reigning Social Credit government. Following his personal defeat at the polls in June, 1959, and the failure of the Liberal Party to win more than a single seat, MacEwan stayed on as leader for a short time before resigning in 1960. He returned to civic politics in the fall of 1959 topping the aldermanic polls.

The journal picks up again in April, 1963, and covers MacEwan's successful mayoralty campaign in the fall of 1963, and his subsequent two-year term as mayor of Calgary. These entries are interesting, not only because of their insight into civic politics and MacEwan's delightfully humorous anecdotes, but also for their commentary on some of the major civic issues of the time. The entries end in February 1966, soon after MacEwan's inauguration as Lieutenant Governor of Alberta.

He was to spend eight and a half years in that office before retiring in 1974 to continue his active private/public life.

November 2, 1958   The messages of congratulations are coming in. One wire states, "You'll need your mother's faith and your father's courage."
November 4, 1958   Inundated with mail and messages—some from loyal friends, some from would-be friends, some who believe they'd make excellent senators. The news reports have been most kind and generous, in most instances. There are always exceptions: a news release from Edmonton office said that "a lean and lanky westerner, Grant MacEwan, was elected to the post of leader of the Liberal Party in Alberta." In one paper, that

story read that "a mean and lanky westerner . . ." They said it was a typographical error, but there could be some significance in the editor's Conservative leanings.

November 6, 1958 I met Crawford Ferguson in Edmonton and we made plans for a program in the constituencies—in the north at first.

Editor's Note: Crawford Ferguson was a lawyer from Trochu and a member of the provincial Liberal executive.

November 16, 1958 At yesterday's caucus the M.L.A.'s agreed with me that a journey to Ottawa for the National Advisory Council could be very pleasant but more good could be gained for Alberta Liberalism if the new leader went into the north country to do some "grass-roots" work in preparation for nominations. Today, Jim Connors, Liberal organizer for Alberta, and I drove to High Prairie and tried to assess this Grouard constituency.

November 17, 1958 Drove to Falher, Peace River, Fairview and Rycroft. Jim Mann, merchant at Peace River, looks like our best bet there. At Falher, we stopped and lunched at Romeo Desfosses' home. Romeo insists he will not run again and "Mamma" makes it very emphatic that he is finished as an active candidate. Romeo is no Laurier as a speaker, but he does hold the loyalty of the Frenchmen in this area.

Jim relates events in the by-election at which Romeo was first elected in about 1950. Jim Connors and Harper Prowse were in the area and using a certain cross-roads store at which they bought their crackers and cheese as headquarters. The post office was kept in the store and there was every reason to believe the family operating the combined unit was Liberal. There were three votes there. But when the votes were counted on election night, that poll showed only one Liberal and there was reason to believe it didn't come from the store. Said Romeo: "I fix." When Jim met Romeo weeks later, there was a twinkle in the French eyes and Romeo explained. "I fix it for next time. I call and say, 'Mrs. M . . ., I have lots letter complaining about you. People say you run post office for Social Credit.'

" 'But, Mr. Desfosses,' the lady replied, 'Social Credit is not boss of post office; the Liberals at Ottawa—they boss the post office.'

"I say, 'Ah, Mrs. M . . . , that is right—the Liberals can say who has the post office.' It will be all right next time, Jim."

November 18, 19, 1958 Nothing very encouraging about Spirit River constituency, but Grande Prairie looks excellent and Cockshutt agent, Mac Perkins, who may be a candidate there, is a top man.

I discover that I am quite well known in the Peace River—whether that is good or bad. I reminded Jim Connors of the first time I ran for city council in Calgary. It was 1953, some friends were pressing me to be a candidate and I pointed out that I had been in the city less than two years and I wasn't well enough known. The reply I received should have humbled me. Said one of my friends, "Grant, you better run this time. If people knew you better they wouldn't vote for you." Anyway, I ran and won.

November 19, 1958   Returning from Peace River, Jim Connors and I drove until two o'clock this morning and found all the Edmonton hotels full of municipal convention delegates. We finally found beds in the Y.M.C.A., "two for a quarter" kind but they were alright.

Airdrie 4-H Club banquet tonight.

A letter from G.G. of Montreal: Congratulations. Just to prove your intention to substitute red for the baloney the Social Credit party has given Alberta for so long, and that your party isn't just another bum steer, might I suggest a Galloway bull as your emblem.

And another: The best of luck and may you soon occupy the seat which Bible Bill and Broadcasting Ernie sat in with airs of divine smugness.

November 20, 1958   Had a speaking date at noon with the C.P.R. Association and at night with the Canadian Industrial Traffic League.

November 21, 1958   The Calgary City Council was host to the three retiring aldermen, Munson, Dixon and MacEwan. An extremely pleasant dinner affair, dampened only by the coldness of the Mayor's speech which consisted of "Thank you, Grant MacEwan; thank you, Ernie Munson; thank you, Art Dixon."

November 22, 1958   Two letters in today's mail make a striking contrast. One writer states generously: "I'll work like hell and never ask any more reward than the satisfaction of seeing the Social Credit hypocrites out of office." The other letter, less benevolent: "Upon election of the Liberal Party, I would be glad to head a system of your government or accept anything at the level of deputy-minister." People are different.

November 25, 1958   Jim Connors and I visited High River, Nanton, and Claresholm. The Conservatives have called their meeting at High River for tomorrow and if they carry out the proposed nomination, Ross Ellis, who now sits in the legislature as a Liberal-Conservative will become a contender for the Liberal candidature.

November 28, 1958   My aged Aunt Aggie MacEwan Smith of Guelph writes to tell me of the first time my Grandfather MacEwan went to visit the girl who was to become my grandmother. The latter's Mother Cowan talked to the young man to test his knowledge of politics and then said: "Go home young man till you know more about the government of your country." The next time he called he was ready to proclaim the greatness of George Brown and Liberalism and won the lady.

December 1, 1958   Edmonton all day and an appointment this evening with the 20th Century Women's Club at home of Mrs. Morris. Mrs. A.P. Hunter is the able president. We talked education in Alberta and ate homemade pies of numerous kinds.

December 8, 1958   Were it not for the wives, it would be easy to get good candidates. Women have been obstacles all this day. At a meeting at Val Frey's home in McLennan, while no candidate was in sight, I tip-toed to where Mrs. Desfosses was sitting and whispered my question: "Believe

Romeo would be willing to run if I had your permission to urge him. Will you agree?'' The answer came loud and clear: ''No''—all the people present turned my way, no doubt wondering what sort of proposition I had made.

Later in the same meeting, Al Hardy of High Prairie indicated an interest in being the candidate for Grouard, but he'd have to get the approval of his ''War Department.'' I volunteered to phone Mrs. Hardy, but the ''War Department'' refused to agree.

In the evening, there was the nominating meeting at Grimshaw for Peace River constituency. James Mann, 41 years of age, B.A. from University of Alberta, Mayor of Peace River 1952-56 and presently a Peace River merchant, was nominated but he explained he couldn't accept because his wife refused permission. ''I can't take it without her consent,'' he stated publicly, ''after all, I don't sleep with the Liberal Party.'' Again, I volunteered to speak to the lady. I did and won an extremely difficult victory. Why do the women take such a dim view of politics? It reminds me of an advertisement in a U.S.A. paper, inserted by a defeated candidate: ''I wish to thank all who voted for me and my wife thanks all who didn't.''

After the Grimshaw meeting, I went to the home of Dr. and Mrs. Casper in Peace River, ate Chinese food, saw the jewellery stolen from the house a few days before and returned in an envelope placed under the doctor's office door. I saw Mrs. Casper's young baboon which the doctor introduced as the only Social Creditor in his household.

Some pretty salty characters in this district. I asked Ross from P.E.I. when he came to these parts and he replied, ''Damn it, I was here before they dug the river bed for the Peace.''

Late last night I found a new problem. At 1:30 a.m., a sparrow flew through the ventilator slot of my window at the Falher Hotel. Removing the thing was quite a problem, and I wouldn't want the Conservatives saying that ''MacEwan had a chicken in his room all night.''

December 10, 1958 Good meeting at Grande Prairie, thanks largely to the dynamics of Joe Benoit. Mac Perkins, who was nominated, is 54, born at Carstairs, Alderman for the city of Grande Prairie, machine dealer and farmer.

The prize of the evening was Paddy Croken, P.E.I. Irishman, who rose to nominate Perkins. Paddy's appearance is that of well-groomed Senator and his voice is soft and convincing. ''It is with deep pleasure,'' said the personable Paddy, ''that I submit the nomination of a man who is close to all of us. Everybody respects him and his name is known in every home in and around Grande Prairie. I offer the familiar name of Mr. . . . .'' There was a long and embarrassing pause. Paddy couldn't recall the ''familiar name.'' Appearing worried, he looked at the man sitting beside him and as his lips moved, it was evident he was whispering: ''What the hell is that name?'' Then he got it, or nearly got it; ''Perkins—Max Perkins. Anyway, Max is our man.''

A moment later, Perkins accepted the nomination and explained that he was Mac, not Max.

December 1958 At Saskatoon for the formal appearance of the new book, "Fifty Mighty Men."

December 14, 1958 To Edmonton by train. My eyes were shut when the conductor came by. He tapped my shoulder, saying: "You'd better wake up or people will think you're a Social Creditor."

December 22, 1958 It was an evening with the Association for the Advancement of Colored People as they staged a children's Christmas concert. The youngsters did everything they should not have done, but they were perfectly natural and perfectly delightful.

December 23, 1958 A tour of the Bow River Development, West Block, today, was a most revealing demonstration of the provincial government's recklessness in spending. There, around the village of Enchant, we saw an irrigation project costing in the magnitude of 13 million dollars, which the local farmers do not want. At first the irrigable area was estimated at 60,000 acres. The revised estimate was 45,000 acres. Carl Anderson of E.I.D. says 5,000. If the acreage in water finally reaches 13,000 acres, the capital cost will be $1,000 per acre plus farm costs up to $75 an acre for leveling and preparing. The area does not lend itself to irrigation, and the government was told by people who can speak with authority. Bryce Stringam, in his first speech in the legislature, made it clear but work went forward. Today we saw the strange spectacle of a costly bridge across a ditch at a fence line, and unused; we saw two costly bridges across the same ditch and less than 100 yards apart; and we talked to enraged farmers.

December 27, 1958 Doing some political homework in the Calgary area—phoning all day. It certainly doesn't make one feel like a statesman—but a politician is no good to anybody if he doesn't manage to get elected.

January 8, 1959 Two hundred and twelve people—158 of them being voting members—crowded into the Legion Hall at Olds to nominate a Liberal candidate for the local by-election now announced for February 9. There were three good names put forward, Alex Weir, Ken McLaren and Walter Anderson. The latter, with a great body of support from around Trochu, won the nomination on the first ballot. It was a great meeting.

January 10, 1959 Provincial Treasurer, E.W. Hinman, says it promises to be a rough season on politicians. He called to visit his former campaign manager at Cardston and, in the farm yard, met the man's small son playing with an Indian boy from the nearby reservation. "Are you still a good Social Creditor?" Hinman asked the white boy, and the reply was "Yes." "And what about you?" Hinman asked, turning to the other. "Are you a Social Creditor?" "No," was the curt reply. "It's tough enough just to be an Indian."

January 12, 1959 Met Walter Anderson at Olds and proceeded to call at every place of business in town. The response was generally good, but there is still the core of rabid Manningites. To one who said he would always vote Social Credit, I remarked: "You know, that party wouldn't have survived at all had it not been for Imperial Oil's fortune in striking oil in 1947." The reply, without any hint of humor, was: "Mister, what you don't realize is that if it hadn't been for Social Credit, there wouldn't be any oil in Alberta."

January 15, 1959 My voice has failed me, but nevertheless, managed tonight to speak to about a hundred Liberal workers at a banquet in the City of Lethbridge. Chairman was the inimitable Allan Cullen, the author of the famous convention crack about "Grant MacEwan's latest book—'What I Know About Politics and Women'." What he held aloft as he spoke was a copy of the MacEwan souvenir notebook with totally blank pages.

January 19, 1959 With Earl Hastings issuing the call, an attempt was made tonight to reorganize the Calgary Young Liberals. Loyal Liberal J.D. McLellan is in the hospital with a heart disorder. I saw the old man tonight. He's sure he'll be better because he's sure "the good Lord will let me live to see Social Credit beaten in Alberta."

January 22, 1959 The 200th anniversary of the birth of Robert Burns falls on Sunday of this week. Tonight I sat to eat haggis and other good things with 400 good people at Lloydminster. It was an inspiring audience before which it was my pleasant lot to propose the toast to the Immortal Memory.

January 23, 1959 More haggis tonight and last night's intake is only partially digested. I like the lines:

"You can talk all ye like about Vitamin D

And how it comes frae the squash and the pea,

But gie me a haggis each day till I dee

And you can stick all your vitamins into your err."

The party tonight was at Calgary's North Hill United Church, and over 300 were present for the banquet and program.

January 26, 1959 This is nomination day for the by-election at Olds. The Conservative candidate, having been nominated a couple of weeks ago, withdrew once for "personal reasons," returned to the contest a day later and again withdrew today. It is now a two-way fight with the Liberal, Walter Anderson, 41 years of age from Trochu district, and Social Credit, MacLeod from Sundre. It promises to be a good fight, and Social Credit is about to bring all its Cabinet "big guns" in.

Tonight we had a nomination at Killam for the constituency of Sedgewick. The successful person was Mrs. Mildred G. Redman of Hardisty, born in the state of Washington, resident near or in Hardisty since 1907, presently councillor in the Town of Hardisty, long time director of the F.U.A. She came to the meeting with lots of supporters, and enough ideas for a throne speech. Her acceptance speech, which was supposed to last five minutes, ran to 35 and before the chairman had time to thank her, she was on her feet again, and made another speech of 15 minutes. She lacks nothing in vigor and stamina and should do well.

I told Jim Connors about Hon. John Norquay winning an early Manitoba election with a majority vote of one, after a neighbor's Conservative bull sent a Liberal voter up a tree in the pasture field and kept him there until after the polls closed. Jim replied by telling of an event in the Ottawa Valley in his father's time. Two neighbors were digging a well, one working at the bottom, filling the pails with clay, and the other at the top. It was election day and after the ladder which let one man enter the well was withdrawn, the Liberal realized that his partner at the bottom was a Conservative. Instead of dropping the ladder from his partner's exit at quitting time, the Liberal took off to the voting poll and left the Conservative down the well. After the poll closed, the Liberal returned, dropped a rope down the well for his partner to struggle with, tied the other end to a tree and fled to go into hiding for a day or two. The Liberals won the election with a slight majority.

January 27, 1959 Meeting at Bowden tonight in support of Walter Anderson. Speakers were Anderson, Neil Leatherdale and MacEwan.

Discussion turned to liquor, rising consumption and government profits. I recalled Mike Maccagno's statements in the legislature in 1957: "Liquor is here. If my constituents couldn't get it, I know what they'd do; they've done it before. They'd drink lemon extract. If they couldn't get that, they'd take hair tonic. If that isn't available, they'd drink canned heat or liquid shoe polish and if everything else failed, they'd drink anti-freeze. That's a good drink for cold weather."

Editor's Note: Mike Maccagno from Lac La Biche, like Desfosses, held an iron grip on his constituency. He was the only Liberal to be elected in 1959.

Premier Manning's assessment of it was pointed enough: "Liquor is not necessarily immoral; it's just crass stupidity."

February 2, 1959 To Medicine Hat for banquet of the Western Stock Growers. Six hundred people sat for the dinner. Chairman John Cross was in a hurry and called upon me as guest speaker before dessert was served. Result: 600 people didn't get their apple pie.

February 5, 1959 With customary pomp and fine millinery, the legislature opened—perhaps for the last session before an election.

February 6, 1959 It was my big day with the usual satisfactions and disappointments which go with politics. As Leader of the Opposition, I made my initial speech on the throne debate. It lasted an hour and 15 minutes. This evening at Camrose and saw Ross Gould nominated. The big disappointment of the day was the Liberal defeat at Olds.

February 10, 1959 This was our first Private Member's Day, and we opened with a motion by Abe Miller asking the government to establish a Hansard-like system of keeping a permanent record of debates and proceedings. For the fourth time in four years, it was defeated by the Social Creditors who want no part of permanent records.

February 12, 1959 By way of pleasant digression, I stationed myself in the book department of Hudson's Bay store for an autographing session—

mostly "Fifty Mighty Men"—this evening.

February 14, 1959 Thanks largely to the efforts of Earl Hastings, the Calgary Young Liberals sprang back to life this evening at a banquet in the York Hotel.

February 15, 1959 This Sunday marks the opening of Brotherhood Week, and it fell to the lot of Liberal MacEwan to introduce Conservative Hon. Ellen Fairclough at the rally in the auditorium. She seems a capable and charming person and Anne Shaw (daughter of A.M. Shaw) is her secretary.

February 20, 1959 The provincial budget was brought in tonight. It's a 309 million dollar deal with the prospect of a 48 million dollar deficit—in all respects an election budget. I like Provincial Treasurer Ted Hinman— the best of the Social Creditors—but I don't like deficits, especially in a province which continues to drain millions from natural resources.

March 2, 1959 Talked at noon today to the Edmonton Kiwanis Club on Alberta's Prize Personality. These non-political speaking engagements really afford the best possible political platforms, and I'm accepting all that are offered.

March 3, 1959 Harper Prowse has missed many sittings recently and we were concerned. Today he entered the debate on a Natural Resources Commission at 5 p.m. and rose to those oratorical heights such as this house has never witnessed from any other member.

Editor's Note: Harper Prowse was a lawyer and professional politician. First elected to the House as a soldiers' representative, he went on to head the Liberal Party in Alberta before MacEwan took over. A fine speaker, Prowse is described by MacEwan as "the greatest debator I've ever heard."

March 4, 1959 There was turmoil in the legislature. Mr. Speaker was befuddled and uncertain. The trouble began when Lee Sims, after moving an amendment, was denied the right to include remarks about the main motion. As usual, Hugh John MacDonald, with all the old highland fight and determination, demanded a ruling and in the confusion following, the speaker gave five non-voting Liberals three minutes to vote or be named. After 10 minutes, order was restored and everybody voted.

March 5, 1959 Provincial Treasurer Hinman closed the budget debate. I didn't agree with all he said, but his presentation was one of the most statesmanlike speeches I've heard in the House.

March 19, 1959 As Jim Connors and I drove to a meeting at Wetaskiwin, I remarked that this was probably a "wild goose chase" and I begrudged the time. There was no assurance of a candidate, and the Wetaskiwin organization has shown no life. The meeting was not big, but it was surprisingly encouraging. We left with a new executive and a most promising candidate, Fred McNaughton, lawyer and product of an Eston wheat farm.

March 20, 1959 Under Orders of the Day, various honorable members pointed with pride to groups of constituents sitting in the two visitors' galleries. It was becoming monotonous. Hugh John MacDonald arose, saying, "I would like to draw the attention of the members to my friend sitting in the Mr. Speaker's Gallery." As eyes turned to Mr. Speaker's Gallery, it was seen to be completely empty. I couldn't resist following him, said "I would point with hope to the only remaining gallery—the Press Gallery—I hope those who sit there are my friends."

March 21, 1959 Meeting of the advisory council of the Alberta Liberal Association, at which I took opportunity of presenting a preview of a 12 point action program for use in the forthcoming campaign.

March 24, 1959 In debating my motion to set up a permanent board to advise on educational methods to check the soaring use of liquor, Abe Miller pointed to increased Alberta Sales—from $3,224,144 in 1935 to $63,017,810 in 1958. Concluded that Social Credit had literally driven Albertans to drink.

March 26, 1959 Harper was on his feet and in his best form. I said to Hugh John MacDonald: "If he had taken to evangelism, he'd have rocked the world, and people would never have heard about Billy Graham." Hugh John agreed and replied by note: "They (the Social Creditors) never quite know how to take it—, how to reply—how long it will go on—all of which builds up a great deal of frustration and leads to things having nothing to do with the subject under consideration."

March 28, 1959 I have a letter suggesting that politicians have no conscience. The view, of course, is not new, but I wanted to cite some proof that many politicians have the finest sense of honesty and honor. I thought of Harold McLaughlin when the iniquitous $20 dividend was being debated in March, 1957. It was in caucus, and somebody remarked that opposition to the payment might prove politically unpopular. Harold spoke out: "It may prove politically smart for Social Credit to pay such bribe money, and we might be cutting our own throats by opposing it, but I believe it is morally wrong and I for one would rather commit political suicide than vote in opposition to my conscience." It's nice to look back and recall that every member of the Liberal caucus echoed that sentiment and stood accordingly.

March 31, 1959 "Socialism," shouted Earl Ainsley as Harper Prowse made some remark in the course of a debate today. Harper paused and said: "If I were not restricted to parliamentary language, I'd tell you what I think of your damn fool philosophy."

April 2, 1959 Social Credit members don't like to be reminded of the $21 million dollars spent on give-away dividends and this year the prospect of a $48 million deficit. When we allude to that huge adventure in bribery, the usual reply is that it was the same as the baby bonus. "Just sucker bait—something for nothing," Art Soetaert called the dividend payment of $20 in 1957. From Social Creditor, Art Dixon, came the rejoinder: "Does the honorable member believe the baby bonus isn't something for nothing?" Art Soetaert replied: "It would be difficult to tell a woman who has had six children that she was getting something for nothing."

April 3, 1959 It is wonderful how government lawyers can write confusion into legislation. Until I read Bill 60, an act to amend the municipalities assessment and equalization act, I thought I understood the meaning of equalized assessment. Now I'm not sure. The act says: "equalized assessment means the valuation of ratable lands within a municipality established on a common basis as related to the valuation of the total ratable lands within all municipalities in the province as determined on a similar basis."

April 4, 1959 Took part in Women's Press Club panel at Coste House on how Eye Opener Bob Edwards would get along if he were in Calgary today. There were expressions of doubt about how he would succeed, but complete agreement that Alberta needs a Bob Edwards today.

We released our Twelve Point Liberal Action Program to the press today. We would have kept it under wraps until the election is called, but there is prospect of the Conservatives publicizing their platform, and we wanted to be first.

April 6, 1959 The legislature sat until after midnight to complete its work. The reason for the late hour was one Liberal—Hugh John MacDonald—who occupied two full hours in his analysis of the gas industry. Everybody, including his loyal colleagues, was tired of it, and the conclusion was that he did us no good. He has been a tower of strength through this session, but there are moments when one can understand why the Campbells massacred the MacDonalds at Glencoe.

April 7, 1959 Lieutenant Governor John J. Bowlen, a bit more frail than usual, prorogued the session at 10 a.m.

April 15, 1959 When it comes to political enthusiasm, the French Canadian people can put the Anglo Saxons to shame. Today's nomination convention at High Prairie for the constituency of Grouard was the greatest in my experience. Over 200 people, mostly French, crowded into the hall with seats for 88 and remained for two hours. Three good men were named, Maisonneuve, Wahlstrom, and Richer, with Paul Maisonneuve winning the nomination on the first ballot. He is 40 years of age, a farmer, with a record of six years in the Canadian army. He was the choice of Romeo Desfosses, retiring member.

At the conclusion of the meeting, old timer, Barney Maurice, rose to thank "Father MacEwan" and remark that it was the greatest political meeting he had seen in the North "and I've been here 62 years." Noting that two of the nominees addressed the meeting in French as well as English, he said they had a better command of both languages than a French politician in eastern Ontario who knew French better than English. In faulty English he said: "Don't vote for that other son of a gun who put bigger stumpage on the moose's tail. Vote for me and I promise the poor shall be poor; the rich shall be poor also and me, I'll be well fixed."

April 16, 1959 Our twelve point Liberal Action Program, released two weeks ago, was the product of prolonged study and effort. It began nearly a year ago, was revised following the leadership convention, and again following the advisory council meeting. Its preparation received all the democratic treatments, but today I learned of a meeting of the Edmonton Liberal Association executive held last night at which the desire to change it greatly was agreed upon. The proposal is to incorporate it as Liberal policy to raise pensions in Alberta to $100 a month. The planners haven't thought to find out how many pensioners are presently receiving provincial payments nor what the total cost. I find there were, at March 31, 1959, a total of 32,437 people receiving provincial pensions of one kind or another and the extra cost of carrying out the proposed plan would be one million dollars a month. I think I know how to cope with Social Creditors and Conservatives, but am not so sure about how one deals with some of the politicians within our own party. They forget that we have proclaimed a determination to promise nothing we cannot deliver. I intend that there be no compromise on that.

April 23, 1959 Reg Clarkson was nominated for Calgary Glenmore and made a long speech in support of a more aggressive policy in exporting natural gas. That, at the moment, is popular but it's difficult to know what some people close to the oil and gas industry really want because we are already committed to 10 trillion cubic feet of our gas for export beyond the province—40 percent of the 24 trillion cubic feet of proven reserves. We all favor export, but some of us will continue to argue that the present Social Credit government has been much more considerate of the exporter than the Alberta user who may justifiably ask for more security than he now has, with respect to supply and price. But is a matter of satisfaction that Liberals retain their convictions and individuality, even though the views are in conflict with party policy.

April 25, 1959 At a St. George's banquet arranged tonight by the Eastern Star, I was introduced as: "writer, agriculturalist and naturalist. As a naturalist, he is an ardent bird watcher, spending most of his time nowadays watching those birds in the government at Edmonton."

April 27, 1959 Hugh John MacDonald, bless him, wrote to one of the Edmonton people seeking to win votes at any price and said, among other things: "From the standpoint of the Liberal party, the most important thing is not that we win the next election or any particular election, but that we serve the Canadian public well and properly. If we do this, not only will we be entrusted by the public when the public is prepared to entrust us, but we will be able to maintain that trust continually." That is the essence of statesmanship.

April 28, 1959 Pounding the pavement and knocking at doors in Calgary North this evening. It's hard work after two or three hours but the reactions are interesting. One man will be full of enthusiasm for the Liberal party; the next will have a Social Credit silence and one of my men tonight—a middle-aged man with the appearance of normal intelligence—said: "I've never cast a vote in my life, and think I never will." I questioned him mildly, learned that the reason was not in any religious beliefs, but simply that "voting is just a farce." I asked what substitute he had for democracy, and he confessed he had nothing to suggest.

May 5, 1959 In an Alberta constituency in which three parties have now nominated—one neighbor asked another: "What do you think about the candidates?" The reply was: "The more I see of them, the more thankful I am that only one can be elected."

May 7, 1959 Bill Jones was nominated to contest Edmonton Norwood. Earlier in the day I met an insurgent Edmonton group wanting us to promise the moon—$100 a month pensioners and so on—but with help from Harper Prowse and Abe Miller, the dreamers conceded that it could be achieved only by deficit financing, cutting back existing services or new taxes.

May 9, 1959 A lady in Calgary North flattered me by wishing I would break my leg. I was knocking at doors this afternoon, unexpectedly called at the door of this lady who is in the employ of the Conservative party. Premier Manning announced the next provincial election tonight. It will be June 18.

May 11, 1959 The turmoil of campaign began this morning. We have 32 candidates nominated and today we have lined up 10 more meetings.

May 17, 1959 At Lethbridge to give the luncheon address to Alberta Junior Chamber of Commerce convention. Thinking that MacEwan, in the midst of a campaign might fail to be present, the J.C.'s arranged for a stand-by— Solon Low, leader of the Social Credit party of Canada. I was glad I was able to carry out the obligation to speak.

May 23, 1959 Jim Connors and I drove from Edmonton to Lac La Biche for one of those great north country nominations. They came at two and remained till six, nominated Mike Maccagno, then returned 100 strong to Mike's cabin after supper and stayed until midnight. Before starting for Edmonton, Mike took me out on Beaver Lake and gave me a chance to catch two pike. Mike's performance on this nomination day was excellent. His half hour speech was a far cry from the first one he made in the legislature in 1955. And the Lac La Biche people love Mike.

May 25, 1959 It's not often one must argue to discourage a man from being a candidate in an election in this age, but it happened today. We need a candidate for Calgary Southeast. I learned of Mr. X who was ready to take the nomination and joyously invited him to come to the office. In appearance he was quite impressive and he seemed a man of purpose. Moreover, he had a hearty dislike to Social Credit and it's hypocrisy. My words were loaded with encouragement—until I began to get the full story—his wife left him, police picked him up and he spent 10 years in the mental hospital. What a let down. Then my greater problem was to explain why, in view of the possible high cost to himself, he should not consider being a candidate. I breathed more easily when he agreed.

May 28, 1959 I was knocking on some doors tonight. One home-owner who recognized me greeted me with: "No use you baby-kisser coming here now. We expect our first baby next week. You can come back then."

Phyllis Cline MacEwan at Priddis, 1959

May 31, 1959 Jim Connors and I started at noon for Grande Prairie in the Peace. Along the way we were to take in a Sunday evening meeting west of Morinville for Art Soetaert, but there was near tragedy. With rain falling and our car moving at 50 miles an hour, we hit a ditch and a couple of feet of water, west of Morinville. Miraculously, we did not roll over. I went on to the meeting with Art Soetaert while Jim remained to see the car returned to the road by tractor.

June 1, 1959 Leaving Art's meeting at 10 p.m. we drove all night, checked in at the hotel in Grande Prairie at 6:30 a.m., went to bed and was visited by Cliff Wright and candidate, Mac Perkins, 30 minutes later. It was a sleepy but otherwise good day and ended at Steve Tachit's meeting at Fairview at night. There were 80 or 90 at Steve's meeting and we ended the day feeling that something was really stirring at the Peace River grass roots.

June 2, 1959 Meetings at Manning in the afternoon in support of James Mann and at McLellan at night for Paul Maisonneuve. At Manning at 11:45, Jimmy Mann, after trying to get a radio message to me that I was to speak at Rotary in Peace River, picked me up and whisked me to luncheon. It was said to be 76 miles but we were at the table in an hour and five minutes. I talked on non-party politics and enjoyed it even on an empty stomach. After Jimmy Mann's afternoon meeting, a chap who was totally deaf wrote on a card, "Damn good speech."

June 3, 1959 It was a bad night. After last evening's meeting in McLellan, we started to Edmonton. At 4 a.m., somewhere south of Whitecourt, the differential shaft broke and fell with a great racket. We were set afoot in the remote north until a fellow with a truck came that way and pulled us to Sangudo. Here I left Jim to seek repairs and hitch-hiked to Edmonton. My ride was on a truck loaded with pigs. This afternoon at Wetaskiwin and tonight at Rimbey, then to Calgary and another late night.

June 4, 1959 Two phone calls greeted me at an early hour—one from a pensioner who said he needed false teeth. If I would see that the government bought him the teeth he would promise me his vote. The other call was from a woman who had just been informed that Grant MacEwan had once been run out of Saskatchewan for embezzlement. "Is it true or false?" she enquired. Raymond for a meeting in the afternoon, Lethbridge at night and again arrived back at Calgary at 3 a.m.

June 5, 1959 Banff at noon to talk to 500 delegates to Canadian Purchasing Association, and Victoria School at night to give graduation address. It was a day of backhand politics.

June 6, 1959 Ted Duncan announced to a householder that he is the Liberal candidate. Said the citizen: "If you were St. Peter running for that party I wouldn't vote for you." Ted replied: "If I were St. Peter, I wouldn't be running in your constituency."

June 8, 1959 At Abee in afternoon and Stettler at night. At the latter meeting, Liberal candidate Henry Kroeger told about his birth in Europe, boyhood days in Moscow and his sense of gratitude for life in a land of freedom. The audience loved it.

June 10, 1959 At Edson for afternoon and Stony Plain at night. At former, we were reminded that Social Credit Wilmore had told the local woodsmen to herd sheep if they didn't like things as they were, and now, just yesterday, Conservative Horner M.P. suggested they grow blueberries and cranberries.

At Stony Plain I talked about Social Credit's failures in dealing with forest fires. A Social Creditor arose, said 30% of forest fires are caused by lightning. "What could the government do about that?" A voice from the back roared: "Put 'em out."

June 11, 1959 In the afternoon we were at Daysland, Killam and Hardisty—and at night at Provost.

June 12, 1959 Attended a Farmers Picnic at Boyle.

June 13, 1959 Camrose for afternoon and Didsbury at night. This ends the campaign tour. Jim Connors and I have driven 4,500 miles in the past two weeks, most of it at night.

June 15, 1959 Two forums and a reception, all called at 8 p.m. but managed—almost—to be in three places at once.

June 18, 1959 Since January 1, I spoke at 101 meetings (38 of which were non-political), did 10 radio talks, 8 T.V. appearances, travelled 4,500 miles with Jim Connors in a two week period, knocked at 3,000 north Calgary doors in spare time, and tonight saw the Social Credit party swept back into power in an overwhelming landslide. Of 65 seats, 61 were to Social Credit, one to Liberal Mike Maccagno, one to Conservative Ernest Watkins, one to Independent Frank Gainer and one to Independent Social Creditor Ainsley. It was the political spectacle of the generation.

1963

Life is a strange mixture of black and white, and nowhere will a person encounter more striking extremes of joy and sorrow, headaches and thrills, bouquets and brickbats than in public service at the civic level. There, close to the people, close to the wallets from which taxes are paid and close to the garbage can problems, politics can be at its roughest. Backbenchers in the House of Commons say they are often bored. In big city politics where most citizens have telephones, there is no chance of boredom. Some day, God willing, I will own a home without a telephone.

Three of my aldermanic friends who were threatened with lawsuits in 1963, know what I mean by occupational hazard. Of course, Calgary Council, which held its first meeting following incorporation in 1884, in Clarke's saloon, has never been noted for tranquility.

April 8, 1963   Federal election day, with Harry Hays, Mayor of Calgary, being elected over alderman Conservative Jack Leslie in Calgary South. What will this do to city council? Rumor has it that Hays will go to the Cabinet to take the agricultural portfolio.

April 29, 1963   Hays, having been named Minister of Agriculture in Prime Minister Lester Pearson's government, called the aldermen together to a private meeting at 1 o'clock today to ask how he should handle his city responsibilities. Most aldermen favored his retention of the post of mayor to end his term, next 16th of October, even though in name only. The chief reason expressed was that he was familiar with the proposed C.P.R. redevelopment scheme and should see it through. It was agreed that we'd have aldermen serving as both deputy and acting mayor for the remaining months, with the Acting Mayors taking the regular mayor's salary. Money seemed to be quite a big factor in the decision.

May 28, 29, 30 and 31, 1963   Attending the Federation of Mayors and Municipalities in Toronto. A big, but not very valuable, assembly with more of food and drink than originality.

June 10, 1963   Hon. Harry Hays has seen fit to submit his resignation as mayor of Calgary and council was today faced with the terms of the City Act which force the naming of a new mayor from members of council to complete the present term. At the council meeting, Ald. Mack was acting mayor and he and Ald. Ballard, Ho Lem, Starr and MacEwan indicated willingness to let names stand for the office. Retiring from the chamber, straw votes eliminated Ballard, Ho Lem, Starr and then Mack, leaving MacEwan to take office on July 1.

June 21, 1963 Hospital Board met, at which chairman MacEwan submitted his resignation and Ald. Ray Ballard was elected to succeed him.

July 1, 1963 This is the day I am supposed to take over mayor's office, but keeping a promise I made months ago, I am at Swift Current judging horse show.

July 2 and 3, 1963 Still judging at Swift Current, an unfortunate circumstance when I am supposed to be in my new Calgary office, leading a Calgary reporter to note publicly that the city still has a "travelling mayor."

July 4, 1963 Took oath of office from clerk Harry Sales and tried to settle into the new routine. The first committee meeting was that of group named to study the hospital bed situation.

July 5, 1963 Held first press conference, with promise to myself that this will be a daily occurrence as long as the press people are interested. City council this afternoon at 1:30, being advanced because of the regular meeting conflicting with Monday of Stampede. First meeting alright except for some deep resentment because I'm blamed by one or two aldermen for the fact that the old timer who wanted the chairmanship of the hospital board didn't get it.

July 6, 1963 Exhibition and Stampede week seems to start on Saturday and this morning there was the annual breakfast at Hudson's Bay store. In evening to airport to welcome Bob Hope and Jay Silverheels.

July 7, 1963 Morning of the annual Sunday pre-Stampede breakfast at Hays Farm. About 3,000 guests fed and entertained. Later in day to National Pony Club rally at Millarville, and to Max Bell's at night for supper.

July 8, 1963 Opening day of Exhibition and Stampede. My part in parade was ride a Jim Cross polo mare in parade, alongside Hon. Harry Hays. It was good fun and a bit like Father Time escorting the new incumbent in office over the streets.

July 9, 1963 The highlight of this second day at Exhibition and Stampede was the annual Rangemen's dinner at which the C.P.R. plays host to the old salts. Slim Pickens the guest of honor.

July 12, 1963 Took commentary on the livestock parade in front of grandstand—30,000 squirming and shouting kids. Later to Strathmore to meet touring party of provincial deputy ministers of agriculture and accompany to Palliser for civic dinner prior to grandstand performance.

July 27, 1963 One of three judging the Canadian National championships at the Arabian Horse Show in Calgary. Later in day, at city hall to receive Bishop of York and present him with city gift.

Editors Note: Many subsequent entries refer to the proposed C.P.R. relocation scheme. The dream of former mayor, Harry Hays, this project was probably the most controversial in MacEwan's mayoralty term. Basically, the scheme called for the C.P.R. to lift its tracks in favour of a location close to the Bow River.

The vacated land was to be redesigned with the city spending some $10 million. The proposal was fraught with problems and changing stipulations by the C.P.R. and while supported by powerful business and press groups, it never held great sway with the general public.

August 9, 1963 We have this day started the city C.P.R. development negotiations which, we hope, will lead to relocation of the tracks now severing this city and rendering almost a hundred acres of land at city centre tax-free for the past 80 years. They call it a 35 million dollar undertaking. The city's cost in acquiring land, renovating bridge, and building a new parkway will cost something like eight million. It promises to be a highly controversial issue, however, partly because many people do not trust the railroad company. The C.P. negotiators are Rod Sykes, Herb Pickard and Fred Joplin.

August 15, 1963 At 12 o'clock noon today I attended at the village of Montgomery to accept the keys of the place as a formal mark of its incorporation into City of Calgary. This city thus increased its population by another 5,000.

August 17, 1963 Millarville Fair, a great experience, in some ways more satisfying than a day at the mighty Calgary Exhibition and Stampede.

August 20, 1963 Played host to the Soviet Ambassador to Canada who happened to be touring the west. We visited Sandy Cross Ranch to inspect the Shorthorns and the Dr. Duffin Arabian farm. The ambassador talks practically no English and I talk no Russian, so we had our problems. He told me, in a rather perfunctory way, Russia has another big wheat crop. Hon. Harry Hays, going to Europe next week, hopes to be well received in Russia and asked me to take the best possible care of the visiting Russians.

September 3, 1963 Attended breakfast at Hudson's Bay store and then officially opened the new cafeteria by burning the H.B. Company brand on the wood panelling of the wall, also burning the MacEwan brand, Rainbow Bar, on a leather for display. Manager Owen Funnell directed operations.

September 6, 1963 Opened Calgary House Builders' Show of Homes in Lakeview, doing it by sawing my way through a hardwood door, and then being presented with the good saw.

September 10, 1963 In conveying greetings to the National Convention of Jewish women, I found it one of the most pleasant parties I've attended and Mrs. Harry Cohen of Cape Breton, the national president, is a person to remember; fine personality, great conversationalist and one with the highest ideals. One of the Maritime universities conferred an Honorary Degree on her.

September 13, 1963 In Edmonton to discuss civic matters with Dr. Donovan Ross and Trade Minister Rierson.

September 14, 1963 It looks as though I must allow my candidature to stand for the mayor's office on October 16 next. Art Smith announced his candidature long ago, presumably to keep all others out of the contest and secure acclamation. I wondered why anybody wants to be Mayor of Calgary, but it's a sad state of affairs if and when there is no contest for the office. A few friends are pressing me, most of them warning that I may not be able to win the round, but it is my duty to try. Perhaps they're right. It's not popular at home, but I think I'll be a candidate.

This morning I invited Bruce Watson and Carl Nickle to my office to talk about it, and Bruce agreed to be chairman of a committee. He introduced the discussion by looking at Carl and me and remarking: "I imagine we three are the loneliest people in Calgary at this minute." The rest of us knew what he meant, inasmuch as the election is less than five weeks away, and we have no organization, no headquarters, no campaign funds, and not even sure we have many friends. But I promised my two friends I'd announce my entry into the mayor's race not later than Tuesday of next week; that would be four weeks and one day before the election. Don MacIntosh phones to say that I could be certain of only one thing: "If you don't run, you'll never win an election."

September 14, 1963 This evening the members of council attended a testimonial dinner for Harry Hays and Dudley Batchelor, the latter retiring from the post of chief commissioner at the end of October.

September 17, 1963 I announced today that I'd be a candidate for mayor on the 16th of October. They tell me on the street that the odds are five to one against me.

September 18, 1963 Art Smith announces his committee which includes many of my Liberal "friends." It looks like a powerful committee. But there is an undercurrent of encouragement from people who are saying: "Art is going to win, but I'm voting for you."

September 21, 1963 Today my committee has grown to five, Bruce Watson, John Ayer, who will be campaign manager, Mel Shannon, Carl Nickle, Nick Taylor, and Hardy Salter. The committee met this morning and did not seem totally discouraged. But still, we have neither campaign headquarters nor funds. So far there has been only one offer of financial assistance.

September 27, 1963 Turned the sod for a new Simpson-Sears development on Macleod Trail. Publicity—I'm doing fine. Perhaps the news columns will help to offset the high-priced paid advertising I can expect from my opposition. As of today, we have a campaign headquarters, at corner of 1st St. and 8th Ave. S.E.

September 29, 1963 To church meeting today, a farewell at cathedral for the dean who goes to the west coast.

September 30, 1963 Council meeting and for the mayoralty candidate in the chair, a rough one, made rough by two Smith supporters. But I managed to maintain composure, and it may have been all right.

My key supporters have been announced, nominating signers and others: Bruce Watson, John Ayer, Carl Nickle, Nick Taylor, Hardy Salter, Rev. Robert Simpson, Harvey Wylie, Ross Alger, Emanuel Krause, Leo Chikinda, Mrs. Rose Wilkinson, Sam Helman, Clarence Mack, Florence Thorpe and so on.

October 2, 1963 Good meeting tonight at St. Joseph's Parish Hall, ostensibly on C.P.R. but with strong political undertones. After meeting I caught late plane for Ottawa to intercede on behalf of Calgary bidder's tender for the $30,000,000 heavy water plant to be awarded.

October 3, 1963 Ottawa. Saw Hon. Harry Hays, Jack Pickersgill, Judy LaMarsh, and others. Just non-committal receptions, but I've done what I can. It seems Nova Scotia's bid for the plant is being favored, notwithstanding the fact that it will be fuelled by subsidized Cape Breton coal.

October 4, 1963 Back home for official opening of the new Glenmore Causeway. A lovely afternoon, a good crowd and a pleasant ceremony with Hon. Gordon Taylor present to take part.

October 7, 1963 I received the unsolicited support of Calgary Labor Council, thanks perhaps to Leo Chikinda. I have been accused publicly of "a deal" with Labor. The Labor Council replied: "This is ridiculous. We say here and now that Labor is not asking or expecting any consideration if Mayor MacEwan is elected . . . We feel Mayor MacEwan is the better man for mayor. . . . Mayor MacEwan has conducted himself as a responsible citizen in his campaign, not attempting to slur anybody, which is commendable, and we know he will carry this same attitude into city hall. When citizens stop and compare the compaign performances, the choice for mayor is obvious."

October 8, 1963 Coffee parties, one a day, and the candidate doesn't drink coffee. But the way friends are rallying for me fills me with gratitude and wonder.

October 11, 1963 Last council meeting before the election. Not as stormy as I expected.

October 12, 1963 Opened Foothills Curling Rink, Montgomery.

October 13, 1963 One-hour opinionnaire session over CKXL with Art Smith. Almost end of campaign.

October 15, 1963 The mayoralty candidates met at Downtown Kiwanis at noon today for the last time. I'm impressed by the supreme confidence of Mr. Smith. As his mother said to me a few evenings ago: "We've been in these campaigns since 1951 and we always win."

October 16, 1963 Election day. My friends are more numerous and more wonderful than I could have realized. Polls closed at 8 p.m. First returns about 8:35 showed MacEwan well up. Looked too good to be reliable. The lead was not only maintained but bettered, and in the end I was the winner with a 13,000 majority. Can't explain it and will not try to explain. But it was a great thrill.

October 17, 1963 Yesterday I packed up my stuff at city hall office. Today, I unpacked. New aldermen elected: Mark Tennant, Roy Deyelle, Dave Russell and Walter Boote. Could be a good council. First phone call: "I worked for you. Can I charge my taxi bills to your account?"

October 21, 1963 Organization meeting of city council and, of course, the swearing in operations.

October 24, 1963   Heather arrived home after her absence on world-circling tour of about a year and quarter. She always looked good to me, but after this long period of absence, she looked better than ever.

November 2, 1963   My friends are still laughing at what Johnny Hopkins reported, correctly, about the mayor of Calgary being stopped in early morning by the police. It was a few minutes before 6 a.m. and I was, as usual, getting the bus on Elbow Drive. It was dark. The police car passed on the opposite side of the street, officers looking my way as if to wonder who would be out at such a bad hour, carrying a black bag. At the intersection, the car made a U-turn and came alongside me. A flashlight was directed at me and a question, "What you doing here?" "I'm on my way to work," I replied. "Where do you work?" was the next question and at this point, the second cop in the prowler car recognized me and hastened to salute me with, "Good morning, Sir. Is there some place we can drive you?" I replied with thanks and said I'd catch my bus about as usual. The story has been printed across the country, even in the *New York Times*, I'm told.

November 19, 1963   Welcomed the Alberta Social Credit League and ventured that it was my first invitation to the august gathering.

November 20, 1963   To Regina by T.C.A. this evening, there to be met by Mr. Justice and Mrs. Brownridge and driven to Moose Jaw for 60th anniversary of city. A pleasant banquet with Mrs. Muirhead, age 92, sitting below me and muttering that she had changed my diapers lots of times.

November 22, 1963   President John Kennedy shot. Word came at noon and the first reaction was that it was another silly rumor. But the news was quickly confirmed, and then, that he was dead. The city hall flag was hoisted to half-mast at once, and letters were dispatched to the U.S. Consul-General in Calgary and to White House. And, as might have been feared, some anti-Americans couldn't hold their tongues and protested the lowering of our flag.

November 27, 1963   To retire Chief Commissioner Dudley Batchelor, we presented a donkey cart and various other things in token of his departure.

November 28, 1963   As a step in furthering the city—C.P.R. redevelopment deal, we met B.J. Showell of Toronto and J.L.S. Crossley of London. No progress until the C.P.R. people were absent, then the problem was resolved quickly with respect to the building of Bow Village.

December 1, 1963   MacEwans and Lyles went to the ranch for an evening in the woods with a big fire. The full moon added the needed touch, and the local coyotes added their notes of music.

Editor's Note: Referred to here is Pete Lyle and his wife Dorothy. He had served on city council and was probably MacEwan's closest friend in Calgary.

December 11, 1963   MacEwan and John Steel visited Edmonton to interview Premier Manning re. legislation for ratification of proposed city—C.P.R. development.

December 12, 1963   Testimonial dinner for Rose Wilkinson, age unknown, but who served on city council for 20 years, 1926 to '45, also in the provincial legislature for 19 years. It's quite a record so soon after Mrs. Emily Murphy won her point to establish women as "persons" in the laws of Canada. Old Rose, as I discovered long ago, makes a better friend than an enemy, but she has been a remarkable person, and I was glad to say so.

December 13, 1963 To Vancouver this afternoon for an evening date with the B.C. Horsemen in a conference. My main part was at the evening banquet, but the best pleasure was sleeping at the sea-side home of Gordon and Mrs. Dudley whom I first met at Washington State University horse shows where Gordon was the horseman.

December 16, 1963 City played host to the visiting Czechoslovakian hockey team. They talk no English, and I talk no Czech so we were inhibited banquet companions.

December 20, 1963 Helped Ernie and Mrs. Starr celebrate their 50th wedding anniversary. Norman Libin and son Leon today proposed a hospital emergency plan which I like and must follow. It consists of using a nursing home with 152 beds at 8th Ave. and 33rd St. S.W. presently being built as an emergency hospital.

December 21, 1963 Max Foran and Pat Treacy arrived. They flew out of Sydney, Australia on the longest day of the year with temperature of 80 above, into the shortest day here with sub-zero temperature. But these Australians seem hardy fellows. After they registered at Trade Winds Hotel, they came out carrying their top coats over arms and insisting it is not cold.

December 28, 1963 It was Heather's big day. At 5 o'clock, she was married to Maxwell Foran of Sydney, Australia; the Rev. Lethbridge of Riverview United performing. Pat Treacy of Sydney was best man, and Heather's attendants included Judy Dundas, Audrey Cowan who came from Australia, Joy Bennion Grant and Gay Cusson. Reception dinner at Palliser for about 150 followed, with Pete Lyle proposing toast to bride.

December 30, 1963 Today we met Mr. Kennedy of Federated Co-ops, Saskatoon, to try explaining why his company should build its proposed 15 million dollar fertilizer plant at Calgary. We'll know in a month if our salesmanship is good or not.

January 12, 1964 Crucial meeting with Dr. Donovan Ross on Calgary's hospital bed shortage. Calgary will get 85 added beds at Baker Memorial with possibility of more at Belcher if the federal authorities agree. And we formally proposed a three-year lease of the Cedars Nursing Home, now under construction, for a 152-bed temporary hospital. Libins, who are building it, would add two or three surgeries and rent all at about the rate of interest on their investment.

January 14, 1964 Com. John Steel and I flew to Saskatoon to interview Federated Co-ops re the proposed 18 million dollar fertilizer plant we hope will be brought to Calgary.

January 16, 1964 Crucial meeting between members of city council and

Ian Sinclair of C.P.R. re proposed city—C.P. redevelopment plan.

January 17, 1964   Second long and crucial meeting with Ian Sinclair and other C.P.R. people. Still no answer.

January 20, 1964   Third late night meeting with C.P. This afternoon we received an anonymous letter bearing threats against nine members of council, including myself. The letter, lavishly smeared with human excrement, shows exactly where each of the victims will be shot and how many .303 bullets he'll get. I'm slated for three.

January 22, 1964   The last of a series of council meetings in connection with the C.P.R. redevelopment plan. A strange meeting. Various motions, which could have endorsed the plan with certain reservation, were deadlocked, 6—6. Finally, the meeting was adjourned, then a new one called a matter of minutes later when a motion was passed, 8—3, approving the agreement but requiring ratification by the legislature and approval by a majority of Calgary ratepayers in plebiscite.

January 23, 1964   Flew out for Ottawa and Innsbruck.

Editor's Note: This was part of Calgary's bid for the site of the 1968 Winter Olympics for Banff.

January 26, 1964   Took train from Zurich to Innsbruck. A grand trip along foot of Alps. And Innsbruck is a quaint old city with narrow streets and no conscience in the matter of traffic laws.

January 28, 1964   Calgary, along with five other places, made bid for 1968 Winter Olympics. Calgary lost out to Grenoble, France. A huge disappointment to our people.

January 29, 1964   Official opening of Winter Olympics, with 60,000 people present on the mountain-side bowl for the arrival of the torch and the presentation of athletes from 36 lands. This afternoon we went to one of the sites northwest of Innsbruck. Tonight, saw Canada and Switzerland play hockey with Canada winning 8—0.

January 30, 1964   Saw men's downhill skiing and late in day, flew out to Munich where I had a good visit with Karl Wohlfahrt and daughter from Landsburg. He is a potential Calgary industrialist and very encouraging when I told him of the abundance of cement, wood material of the poplar order and availability of help. He has just returned from Turkey where he was recruiting workers for his plant.

February 4, 1964   Flight from London to home. Never a ripple in the atmosphere until almost over Calgary when we flew into gales and were forced to go back to Regina for a few hours.

February 12, 1964   Police Commission with most time spent on wage negotiations. It seems that organized labor almost runs municipal government these days.

February 15, 1964   Attended Junior Achievement breakfast and gave out a questionnaire to test the reaction of these teenagers to elected public service. In general, the youngsters from the United States had a higher respect for politicians and political service than the Canadians.

February 17, 1964 Council meeting. Mark Tennant objected to the mayor travelling second class on his recent trip overseas. It's not fit and proper, he said.

February 20, 1964 Special meeting today to find a basis upon which the city could make better use of the Veterans' Belcher Hospital. Attending were Dr. J. N. Crawford of D.V.A., Ottawa and Dr. Donovan Ross, Minister of Health, Edmonton. Legion people present objected but it looks as though we made some progress toward takeover to be handled by a new Metropolitan Calgary Hospital Board.

March 8, 1964 Again, this Sunday evening, Heather, Max and I skated. It is a new and not-very-encouraging experience for Max who is new on skates, but it promises well as something we can do together.

April 16, 1964 Date at noon with Victoria Men's Canadian Club and after-noon with Women's Club. 475 at latter. Before leaving Victoria, a real estate man drove me north along Saanich Pen. to look at some ocean front proper-ties. Look good, especially when I think of the grief we've had lately at city hall.

April 21, 1964 Sold my Millarville quarter through Stuart McRae to Jim Cross for $13,500 net.

April 22, 1964 Saskatchewan election and it looks as though the Liberals under Ross Thatcher have at last unseated the CCF.

April 23, 1964 Phone called me from bed to be told the caller was having severe static on his radio due to something the city electric light department was doing. Could I please have it attended to before an 11 o'clock show came on.

A few days ago a call came from Boston to me. Are you the mayor of Calgary? Yes, I said to the lady calling. Well, will you please help me locate so-and-so in Calgary because he's the father of my last child and doesn't know it.

May 9, 1964 The industrial triumph of the decade was announced today that Western Co-operative Fertilizers Ltd. will build its $21 million plant here. We've been working on it a long time and knew that all other western communities wanted it as eagerly as we did. It will be 320 acres south of Ogden, will employ 185 people and be in production in midsummer, 1965.

May 22, 1964 Opening of Tom Baines bridge beside St. George's Island. Tom cut the ribbon and was touched by the experience. Tom leaves the ser-vice at zoo after 35 years of faithful service.

June 2 and 3, 1964 Federation of Mayors and Municipalities Convention, Regina. On 3rd, I had the assignment to speak at noon luncheon on topic "The Old West and The New."

June 5, 1964 John Steel and I at Edmonton to interview C.N.R. Vice-President, Roger Graham, about getting through on C.N.R. land for parkway in connection with C.P.R. project, and were told the only solution would be for city or C.P. to buy the C.N. out on its present 28 acres between 6th St. and the Elbow and relocate everything. Looks like a $5 million operation for somebody. Council will not like this and even though it affects C.P. more than city, nobody will think to blame C.P.R. for its failure in negotiating more successfully with C.N.

June 8, 1964 Council with large part of meeting given to review of C.P. problem. Everybody sick of it.

June 17, 1964 Five of us—Aldermen Tennant, Ballard and Starr, Commissioner John Steel and I took jet to Montreal for a showdown visit with the officials of C.N. and C.P. with respect to the proposed city—C.P. redevelopment plan.

June 18, 1964 Visit with Mr. MacMillan of C.N. was most encouraging. We found him understanding and gentlemanly. Our next call was at C.P. where we met president Crump and vice-presidents Emmerson and Sinclair. They were not helpful. If we want parkway east of 6th St. East, they will give us air rights and we can build an elevated parkway. It looks like a five million dollar undertaking and will not be well received either by council or the public.

June 22, 1964 Committee to the East reported to council and saw the majority of aldermen vote to refuse to re-execute agreement. It looks like the end of the scheme for the present. It would have succeeded if the C.P. had not been so damnably greedy and had others doing their negotiating.

July 14, 1964 Turned sod for the first Calgary winery to be built on Blackfoot Trail. I'm committed to pressing out the first grapes with my bare feet.

July 15, 1964 It happened again that the same mail brought two letters demonstrating the extremes in which anybody in public life is held; one telling me that I am the greatest mayor in Calgary's history and the other that I am the worst of Calgary's mayors and it will be a good day for the city when my term is over.

July 20, 1964 More than usual "Call the Mayor" messages have been coming by phone. One man called to demand that I stop the army trucks from using his streets at night and "do it tonight." Another was a plea from a youngster, urgent, that I use my influence at once to get the Beatles to come to Calgary. "We kids love them and we don't see how we can live without them." Still another call today from a woman in great distress because a wasp nest has been detected in a tree on her boulevard and her husband was stung. I asked her what action she would suggest, fire department, police or parks department. She didn't have a clue as to what should be done, but "do it fast."

August 5 and 6, 1964 Penticton for Patron of Peach Festival. Very much impressed and everything went as planned except that timing was out and local peaches were not ripe and supplies had to be imported from farther south in the valley.

August 15, 1964   Bowness became part of Calgary by annexation today.
August 26, 1964   The new and extensive Woolco shopping centre opened today.
September 9, 1964   Turned sod for Sam Switzer's new hotel on 4th Ave. and 1st St. S.W.
October 14, 1964   Civic election. 23.8 percent turnout. New aldermen will be Roy Farran, Jack Davis and Adrian Berry. The strongest fight occurred in Ward 6 where Nick Taylor and Charles Smith were defeated by Davis.
October 19, 1964   City council organization meeting. The worst I recall because aldermen wanted to work over the committees before turning them over to the committee to strike committees.
October 22, 1964   *Calgary Herald* opened its new building with the newspaper brass of Canada in attendance. I reminded them in congratulations that the *Herald* is one year older than Calgary and during its 81 years it has "grown in wisdom and in stature, even though not in favor with God and man."
October 26, 1964   Council meeting. The big issue concerned the commissioner's recommendation to accept the offer of the exhibition and stampede board to take Lincoln Park off city hands at cost ($750,000) as soon as we acquire it. Some 200 people came to register protest and council authorized reference back to commissioners for study. The exhibition people are now satisfied they should move there but there will be lots of opposition from nearby residents. The alternatives to Exhibition Park are: industry, satellite air field, residential, and Mount Royal College is interested in a part of it. What may have some bearing on public reaction, there is now a rumor that a packing plant is interested.
Editor's Note: This was another controversial issue. The city had bought the land at a good price and the Calgary Exhibition and Stampede was interested in the site. The city, however, accepted a recommendation from its Planning Department that the site not be used for exhibition purposes. Much of the land is now occupied by Mount Royal College and ATCO Industries.
October 27, 1964   Woman phoned me today to report that she had been molested on the street near city hall. What was I going to do about it? I enquired if she had reported it to police and she said she hadn't because she didn't want the police to know about it—she admitted she didn't want the police to know she was in the city.
November 6, 1964   Cardston was host for breakfast at UAM in Lethbridge. On the table was a pot resembling a chamber pot with sign on it: Reserved for Mayor Grant MacEwan's porridge. There was a special make of porridge for me. It more than half-filled the chamber pot, but I made up my mind I wasn't going to leave any. It was painful slogging but I finished it, much to the amazement of delegates who were watching attentively.
November 6, 1964   Press reports a Calgary man of 76 years charged with being a found-in at a local house of ill fame. One of our aldermen proposes

sending him a letter of congratulations.

November 13, 1964   Today an author's party put on by Modern Press because of appearance on this Friday, 13th—also my 13th book—"Of Hoofprints and Hitching Posts." Autographing at Carmen Moore's tonight.

Police reminding me of the old lady driver who went through a red light on 8th Ave., then, noticing a policeman on the corner, stopped and backed the full distance through the same intersection and displayed all the innocence of a child.

They also tell about a traveller by air from Edmonton who left his plane at McCall Field and took limousine downtown. Obviously half shot, he asked a cop where he would find Granville St. The officer said, "There's no Granville St. in Calgary; there's one in Vancouver." "Isn't this Vancouver?" "No, this is Calgary." "Well, I'll be damned. I thought it was a hell of a short ride from Edmonton."

News from Auckland, N.Z. today tells that John Steel has been appointed general manager of the Auckland Regional Authority.

It will be a great loss to Calgary, but the hounds have been baying for him ever since the C.P.R. deal was under review. In both capacity and integrity, he was far above his critics.

December 3, 1964   At Edmonton for meeting with mayor of that chilly city and Hon. Russell Patrick to get the latter's approval for an inter-city power development based on a thermal plant at Ardley, 20 miles east of Red Deer. Having obtained the grudging approval, we made our first announcement about the big program which would tie Calgary, Edmonton and Red Deer together in generating electric power from coal to be supplied by Dynamic Power which holds the fabulous coal. We expect Calgary Power to cry loudly and tell us of all the reasons why it can't be done. City Council will hear about it formally on Monday and their reaction will be interesting.

December 9, 1964   Flew to Edmonton for first meeting of an inter-city committee to investigate the proposed power development on coal reserves at Ardley. Obtained Alberta Research Council's cooperation and set up a continuing committee.

December 11, 1964   Attended the big Chamber of Commerce luncheon to hear the promoters describe North American Water and Power Alliance—NAWAPA, a hundred billion dollar project.

One of the visiting speakers from California asked me if "Premier Mannix is any relation to Mannix of construction?"

I'm still being called "Mayor MacKay" about twice a month.

Editor's Note: Don MacKay was one of Calgary's more colorful and popular mayors, and held office in the 1950's before Harry Hays.

December 14, 1964   Ottawa to interview Department of National Defence re road needs through Tecumseh, also DOT re McCall Field future and Crown Assets re Lincoln Park.

It happened again as it did when in Europe last February. Then, my T.C.A.

ticket was made out in the name of Mayor G. MacEwan. The word "mayor" wasn't very distinct and the European people who knew the head of civic government only as Büromeister, read my ticket rather consistently as "Major MacEwan". I accepted the new name.

On this trip east, I found again that when the mayor travels, every hotel clerk seeks to unload upon him the most expensive room in the house. It's supposed to be courtesy, but it's really a matter of gouging to find a use for the high-priced accommodation. It's much more economical if a mayor can travel incognito. He'll be able to relax without being pestered by press and hotel attendants expecting generous tips.

December 15, 1964 At 2:13 a.m. today, the House of Commons adopted a maple leaf flag after a long and bitter debate. I sat in the gallery until that 2:13 hour this morning and saw the Liberals win their fight on a vote of 163 to 78. It seemed like a historic moment.

December 18, 1964 Hospital board meeting. The big issue was the suspension of a second-year nurse for speaking boldly on hot line of CFAC in connection with hospital working hours and conditions. Where do you draw the line between discipline and free speech?

January 6, 1965 Members of council and commissioners gathered for a farewell for chief John Steel at Holiday Inn this noon, presented him with a Gissing painting and wished him well in his new post at Auckland, New Zealand. Responding to the presentation, John made something of a "deathbed confession," concerning "that thing which was 'conceived in sin and shaped in iniquity,' " obviously referring to the late city—C.P.R. redevelopment scheme. The commissioners had inherited it and tried to make it work, but as he looks back now, he realized that they should have killed it in its infancy, as soon as possible after the former mayor had signed the Heads of Arrangement. The final approval of the scheme, said John, would have been the greatest tragedy that could have befallen Calgary and he wanted to speak out clearly on this before leaving.

January 7, 1965 Percy Page, Lt.-Gov., yesterday said in presence of a reporter, that he will be finished next fall and if he had the choosing, he'd pick Grant MacEwan from Calgary to follow him. The story found its way onto the wires and today has been mildly embarrassing for me, but far more so for P.P.

January 9, 1965 This marks the end of the coldest four-week period I recall in Calgary. Cattle and pheasants are reported to be dying and the city crews are working overtime to keep frost out of the operations. Happily, the Bow River ice has become consolidated and is behaving well. City streets are not good and it's too cold for salt to work. Pete was telling me about when he was out with a steam engine thawing out a frozen main. He was about perished and didn't want to go far to a men's room. His colleague said: "Step into that cloud of steam and you will be completely hidden." Pete did and found it was working fine until the sinful fellow worker shut the steam off and left Pete exposed to everybody on the street. Calgary, it may be said, however, is the only place in the world where the weather can change as fast as the traffic lights. It doesn't blow like at Lethbridge where they tell the direction of the wind by hanging a logging chain on a fence and watching which way it points like a semaphore. The only place where you can play golf and ski the same day. The only place offering the novelties of both Siberia and California. While Lethbridge has a windy city and Edmonton a frosty city, Calgary's weather is always unusual.

January 11, 1965   The Scottish curlers are here and I welcomed them tonight. One old Scot said: "There are many MacEwans in my part." "Are they all thugs?" I asked, to which he replied: "Aye."

January 14, 1965   Guest speaker at Saskatchewan Farm and Home Week banquet—University Personalities of Other Years. It was the same role I filled exactly 25 years ago this week.

January 24, 1965   Sir Winston Churchill died at age 90. My message: "From the news of recent days, we knew Sir Winston was close to death but, still, the word of his passing casts a pall of shock and sadness over this community, as over communities in all of the civilized world. More than any man of his generation, he captured the admiration of people in all lands. In war years he seemed to be precisely what the struggling western world needed and men said: 'Surely, he has come into the Kingdom for such a time as this'.

"His body was strong; his words were inspiring, his spirit was unbeatable and, to the end of time, his great record will be recounted with admiration. At this moment, so soon after his passing, the citizens of Calgary would stand with me in reverent expression of respect and gratitude and sorrow; but thankful for the privilege of knowing him as all people of the free world knew him."

February 1, 1965   This being written from a padded cell after this day's series of meetings, including a 5 1/2 hour council meeting.

February 2, 1965   To Banff in No. 1 car to see if Charlie Beil will make up something exclusive for use as souvenir of Calgary. He proposed a buffalo skull in plaster.

February 17, 1965   Tisdale for Hudson Bay Route Association. I was banquet speaker and threw out the challenge that the association rewrite its constitution to end this annual threshing of old straw, and take promotion of the entire north as its responsibility. Tisdale proved one thing: that a town of 2,900 people can turn out the welcome and friendliness to match the performance of any city.

February 22, 1965   Yesterday, I met a group of voluntary workers, some of whom have been giving their time—one full day a week—for years to a charitable purpose, doing it without looking for reward of any tangible kind, not even seeking public recognition. It's nice to know that their kind survives for "of such are the Kingdom of God."

February 23, 1965 A liquor company representative called today, left a bottle of Windsor whiskey and asked that I stand for a picture which they can use in advertising in U.S. for their brand of Alberta whiskey. "Mr. Calgary" had to say "no."

March 4, 1965 One nice thing about being mayor is in the fringe benefits— free advice, for example. If I had to pay at consultant's rates for all the advice I get, a thousand dollars a week wouldn't cover the bill. That would total $52,000 per year and I don't have to report any part of it to income tax.

March 6, 1965 The reward for public service comes, one-third in dollars, one-third in valuable experience and one-third in satisfaction.

March 6, 1965 In search of new sources of tax revenue, our aldermen are showing a strong interest in syntax. After all, just about everything else is taxed.

March 7, 1965 We'll never have perfect government until the editorial writers run the country. They're the only ones who are always right. But who ever heard of one running for office of alderman? Last night's prize phone call was from an irate citizen reporting his anger at the city's failure to enforce the sanitation bylaw. What was wrong? Well, he had taken a taxi and when he entered the back seat, there on the cushion were half a bottle of gin and a sanitary napkin. "What you going to do about it," he asked. I enquired if he knew which taxi it was and he admitted he didn't but he wanted something done about it. I asked, "What did you do with the gin?" and he replied: "I drank it. What the Hell do you think I'd do with it?" Evidently, he was not upset about the gin being left. I told him he couldn't have everything just as he wanted in this world.

March 10, 1965 Mayor Wm. Hawrelak of Edmonton unseated by judgement of Chief Justice Campbell McLaurin, because of a land deal involving property bought by the city from a company in which Bill held more than 25 percent of the stock.

March 16, 1965 Transit committee today brought out the best example of unreasonableness in today's city residents. A group in northwest Calgary petitioned for an extension of bus service. It was granted and today some of the same people were back to complain that they did not want the buses running on their streets. Hazard to kids and made added traffic.

March 25, 1965 Aldermen met again re appointment of a chief commissioner. As a result, I will prepare recommendation to council that J. Ivor Strong be appointed.

March 26, 1965 With Commissioner Ian Forbes, drove to Morley to attend the birthday party for 94-year-old Chief Walking Buffalo. Introduced to a Mrs. C. with the words, "Meet the mayor, Mr. MacEwan." The reply was a question: "What, the mayor of Morley?" Somehow, I think it would be fun to be the mayor of Morley.

April 12, 1965 Council today revoked the grocery store license of an individual who, according to police, was convicted on five occasions under

the Indian Act and that between January 4, 1964 and January 25, 1965, purchased 270 cases—each of 36 bottles—of after-shave lotion. The bay-rum
business was pretty good.

April 16, 1965 Phone call at house. "That Grant?" "Yes," I replied.
"Grant who? Grant, the mayor?" "Yes." "Well, will you come down to
the bus depot because I'm in trouble. I can't get my stuff out of this damned
baggage box. My friend has the key and he hasn't come back. I gotta get
the bus to Gleichen." "Who are you?" I enquired. "Johnny Wolflegs,"
he replied. "Will you come down?" "But I have no authority at the bus
depot." "Aren't you the mayor? Well, you're the boss and I gotta get into
this damned box. You have to hurry because I gotta get the bus and I can't
get the bus till I get into this damned box."

May 5, 1965 City budget meeting, 50 million dollar current budget and
16 million dollar capital.

An annoyed woman called to protest Mr. Justice Milvain's judgement on
Early Closing Bylaw. "Why don't you fire all those judges," she said. "They
don't do the right thing and you're the boss and should just fire them."

May 6, 1965 Demand for a local park in north Calgary was accommodated
and Harry Boothman planted trees a few days ago. Today, some of the same
petitioners have asked that the trees be removed because they are spoiling
the view of the mountains.

May 8, 1965 One of our heads of departments was asked how MacEwan
was as mayor, and the reply was "honest and stingy," which pleases me fine.

May 14, 1965 Arbor Day in Calgary. Seven thousand trees distributed to
grade three children and more thousands would be planted by other agencies.

May 15, 1965 Polish Canadian Youth Club Banquet. The Poles surpass
most people in eating and drinking and having fun. Heard about Sid
Buckwald, when accompanying the Quaker hockey team and doing so as
mayor of Saskatoon, in Holland. Wishing to impress the local people at a
banquet, he determined to memorize a few words of Dutch—perhaps Ladies
and Gentlemen. He took the words from the doors of the hotel lavatories—
Ladies and Gentlemen—but after the speech when complimented on the good
performance, somebody said: "But why did you address us as 'Toilets and
Urinals'?"

May 22 and 23, 1965 Painted house.

May 30, 1965 Speaker at the twice annual church service at the old
McDougall Church at Morley. Talked on philosophy from the Tipis.

June 14, 1965 Turned sod for the new 24 St. west bridge complex—a 4
1/2 million dollar enterprise.

June 15 and 16, 1965 Governor General and Madame Vanier in Calgary
making final formal visit.

June 27, 1965 Heather and Max presented me with a Father's Day gift
of an aquarium, equipped and stocked.

July 1, 1965 Heritage Park opening. Spectators were surprised when the

Lieutenant-Governor J.W. Grant MacEwan

mayor didn't miss the last spike in the one-mile railroad.

July 25, 1965 Phone call last night. "Why don't your parks department people roll the lawns at Central Park?" I enquired the reason for the call. "Well, some people have to sleep there and it's damn rough." "But," I said, "they're not supposed to sleep there." "That may be," the party replied, "but when your old lady boots you out and there's no place else to go, a man deserves a level piece of grass in the park." "Has this happened more than once to you?" "Yes, just about every Saturday night. How about getting the grass rolled?"

July 29, 1965 My house phone rang at 5:45 this morning. I was shaving. Phyllis answered and reported that the call was for me. A lady's voice said: "You the mayor? Well, the damned helicopter you authorized for city work has just wakened me from a good sleep and I thought I'd waken you and let you share my misery." I thanked her and told her that I was up and dressed and she'd have to call earlier next time if she wanted to be mean.

August 14, 1965 Yellowknife where I was guest speaker and paid $3 to hear myself speak at dinner.

August 27, 1965 Met Prime Minister Lester Pearson at airport.

August 31, 1965 Refused invitation to be candidate in Calgary North, federal.

September 13, 1965 Announced to city council this afternoon that I had decided against running for re-election to mayor's office. Jack Leslie resigned immediately after to run.

September 14, 1965 Having said to a friend that I could look forward to some freedom after October 13, he asked seriously: "Is your wife leaving you?"

September 19, 1965 Big party at George Ho Lem's new home honoring MacEwan in his retirement from council.

January 6, 1966 Sworn in as Lieutenant-Governor of Alberta, with Mr. Chief Justice Bruce Smith officiating.

January 7, 1966 Bought home at 13845 Summit Drive on offer of $25,000, possession January 20.

First official function, Edmonton Chamber of Commerce annual meeting.

VI
Contemporary Reflections: An Interview 1983

The following transcript of an interview with Grant MacEwan is re-printed unedited and in its entirety. Conducted by Max Foran in the summer of 1983, this interview shows Grant MacEwan at his frankest, and represents a good spectrum of his contemporary beliefs and attitudes. Whether it be his advocacy for environmental trusteeship, the need to preserve our human heritage, or even his thrifty approach to everyday living, Grant MacEwan is impelled by the need to conserve. His well-integrated philosophy is also underpinned by a commitment to purpose. For MacEwan, purpose is the second dominant factor in his life, and as such, he laments on its apparent absence in modern society. He reflects on the past and, in typical fashion, dwells on his future endeavours. Essentially this interview provides documentation on the evolution of a remarkable individual.

Interview with J.W. Grant MacEwan August 8, 1983

Well, I suppose that anybody who has been breathing for 81 years will have some memories, and should have something that he is ready to share with the people around him. I don't know whether what I have got is worth sharing or not. It's been an interesting lifetime and it has changed from time to time. When I look back now, I can see some major reverses in my way of thinking and in my general philosophy.

You know that my background was markedly orthodox. My parents, and particularly my mother, were Scottish Presbyterians, which meant that you really kept the Sabbath; everything that had to be done ceased on Saturday night. If you were going to whistle on Sunday, you whistled a sacred tune. If shoes happened to be dirty, they could wait till Monday. We milked the cows and fed the horses, but we didn't do anything that we could escape from doing on that day. My mother would take the kids to church. My father didn't necessarily accompany us very often. He was somewhat more of a free thinker. He was a man of action. He saw more to criticize in the modern church than mother or any of us did. I think he was ahead in that respect. Yet he had his philosophy and I inherited more of it than for a long time in my life, I realized.

One of Dad's purposes in life was to leave his farm better than he found it. That meant that the fences had to be kept up, and the soil kept free from weeds and that the fertility be maintained. I think that is not very different from the purpose of the young Grecians coming up to citizenship more than 2000 years ago. They committed themselves to a programme of work and athletics, and they took an oath to leave Athens better than they found it. It was for them to figure out how that was to be done. I think today, that most of our people—I don't say this unkindly—feel that the greatest achievement in life is to take as much as possible out of the land, and convert it into money. If the resources are poorer and their bank account is richer, then they are satisfied. But that is not leaving Athens or Canada or Alberta better than we found it. I think my father left his farm better than he found for the next people who came along.

If you want my philosophy in a word, and I guess I can assess it myself, I'm a conservationist. The concept of conservation that I have and which has come to mean a great deal to me, took the place in my thinking of the conventional church-going philosophy of my youth. It was commonplace thinking in those years that if you believed in the Lord Jesus Christ, nothing else mattered. You could exploit the soil; you could overwork your horses. You might get away with it. I tended to accept this philosophy. I was a good church man for a time and as long as my mother was alive, I think she was very happy to think that I took up the collection in Knox Church, did some ushering and was a member of the board. It took up considerable time as I obediently followed the teachings of my mother's family. I had one of the greatest mothers in the world, and today I wouldn't change anything. But it wasn't for me to remain in that line of thinking.

It was when I left Saskatoon that a major change occurred. I had been anticipating it, but I was so involved with the conventional church that it wasn't easy just to walk away. But when I left Saskatoon, I decided that, for a period of time anyway, I was not going to be a regular church attendant. I was going to think this thing over. I did not return to the church, but I needed to find something else to take its place. It was after 1946 that I developed a new concept of purpose.

I always felt that everyone should have a purpose—whether it was to make a million dollars or to be the best farmer in the community or to have the best horses on the road—everybody should have a purpose, and in some way most people do. It can be selfish or it can be noble. It can be something with a good moral foundation. At that time I was looking for a more satisfying link with my Maker. It didn't happen overnight, but took shape gradually.

I came to the conclusion that I could not serve my God better in anything than in conservation; taking care of His garden, His household, His world of nature, His resources, His soil, His trees, His water, His air, His iron ore and so on. Of course this new line of thinking played a degree of havoc with the conventional concept of prayer and the like. My mother was a praying person and raised me to be the same. There was never a break in that and there won't be. But, instead of saying that there is a God of love who demands certain things from His children, I began to determine how I could serve Him in a sensible way.

What has He got to tell me that He would not tell any other person, whether they were raised in the church or not? I was raised in the church, but I guess that a majority of the world's people, at that time, were not raised in the church. I couldn't conceive of a great overriding power that would give me an advantage. The Almighty didn't make any attempt to create all people Presbyterians. He didn't create them with denominational views. There are a thousand denominations with strong convictions. Why should I have an advantage in working out a moral concept or purpose just because I was born within a denominational group?

Basic to all living things is instinct. My instinct and I think, human instinct, points to a higher power—call Him a Great Spirit if you're an Indian, or call Him God if you belong to some other group. I think there is something in humans, if they allow it expression, which is akin to your foal born in the snow three years ago and which was the most helpless thing that ever tried to stand up. But it did, and furthermore, something told that helpless creature where to find some milk. I think there are pointers in my life. Instinct would be one of my working materials—my working resources. Second would be conscience. I think I was born with a conscience. I think everybody is, but that is not to say that it is always given an opportunity to express itself. I think it's there and I think it should be cultivated. Third, there is reason. It may not always seem like very good reason, but it's mine and I inherited it. And with instinct, conscience and a sense of reasoning, I can establish a contact with something bigger than myself.

If I had never heard of doctrines, I think I could have satisfied myself that I was serving a spiritual purpose by looking after the soil, by looking after trees and birds and animals and fellow humans, and my own body, of course. This is part of the God-given resource. So, over the years this concept took form, and it did more for me by far than anything that happened to me when I was going to church. I went to church in a perfunctory sort of way and just like the people around me, we stood at the right moment, we sang hymns with gusto and we put 25 or 10 cents on the plate when it came around and then went home and forgot about the purpose of it all. People must have purpose. I have a completely different purpose to my mother, for example. But it satisfies me and I think it has given me a better spiritual base. I *think* I am ready to be a good steward in His household.

And everybody who is 80 or 81 years should be thinking a little bit about how he is going to meet the day of judgement if there is such a thing. I'm not sure and I don't care.

You're not afraid?

Not afraid! No, No, No! If there's a higher power, I think that perhaps it has been good for me to have been seeking for Him anyway, and *trying* to determine how He would have had me conduct myself.

What about your fellow creatures? How do you see yourself in relation to them and your maker? Do you see yourself in a custodial role?

That's definitely been a big turning point in my life. On the home farm, we kept livestock. Most of the horses worked pretty hard. I think that my father had more sense of feeling for horses than most people had. That's one of my rich memories. I like to think of old Dad when selling the farm, refusing to sell it at the highest price because he was afraid that the man who took it over might not give his horses good care, and he also wanted his horses to stay on the farm. That was an essential. So, instead of selling to the best advantage, he went out and he picked a neighbour and he said, "If you look after my horses and promise me that they will always have a good home, here's a farm that you can have at your own price," which turned out to be about half that which it was worth.

You approve of this?

Oh yes, very much. Apart from horses, we were in the meat business. True, we sold some cream, butter and eggs, but livestock to us was mainly beef and poultry, dressed poultry and maybe some pork. I grew up with the belief that this was part of the Plan, the Divine Plan and that man, according to Genesis, must have dominion over all and could exercise any treatment he chose. He could employ cruelty. As long as the animals were serving his purpose this was all right. This didn't make very much sense to me and I began to do my own thinking. I was in livestock, and I gave some instruction in meats. I did some short course work in farm meats. It bothered me *increasingly*, particularly after the break with the organized or conventional church. It led to a change in my diet.

I have never tried to convert anybody to my new diet, but it was early in my life that I latched onto a few things in the Book of Isaiah. I don't know if Isaiah knew any more about God than you or I. But he was one of the great thinkers. He had a dream. I'm sure he knew that he would never see its fulfillment, but he talked about the day when Man would neither hurt nor destroy God's holy mountain. It seemed to me that Isaiah was taking issue with Genesis and that the human, in his arrogance, had no right to place himself above the Almighty's other children. If there is a God, and I *choose* to believe there is, and if he is a God of love and justice, then He

Calgary Stampede Parade, July 13, 1970.

thinks just as much of one of His children as He does of another, and because one may have a little more intelligence, that is no reason why he should show favoritism.

Is this why I've actually seen you shoo a fly rather than hit it?

Yes, I've had a little trouble in drawing the line, if I do adopt that concept that every living thing has some entitlement. If somebody attacks me in the dark and I have a club handy, I think I should slug him, but I don't think I should go out of my way to kill the grizzly. If the grizzly will leave me alone, I think I should leave him alone. I like Albert Schweitzer of German-African fame, that notable personality who was a scientist, musician, medical doctor and spiritual leader. I can't think of anybody in his generation who could come close to him. But his great concept, of course, was reverence for life and it didn't matter whether it was lowly or high. That fly you speak of or the ant or the bee is in its organization of body, just as wonderful as I am, and maybe even also in its intelligence. I'm not the one to say that it has any less than I have. The organization of a beehive, or an anthill, is beyond comprehension and simply marvelous.

Who am I to say that I am higher just because I'm bigger or just because I've exploited resources more or made more of my opportunities? Who am I to say that I am higher or nearer the ideal citizen on this world? No, I think we are having a few troubles now that stem from human prejudice. I think we'll always have some of that until we embrace the principle of universal equality. We have a record of prejudice in this country, I'm afraid. I think of the way the Hutterites were treated when they came to this country, and still are, to a degree. I think of the efforts that were made to block the Negroes when they were coming in 1910. I think of the way the Japanese were herded off their property in the Second World War without compensation or apology. There are lots of examples and I hope that we continue to fight for brotherhood. Furthermore, I don't think that brotherhood should be confined to humans. You have to make it all-embracing if we are going to develop a concept of compassion and mercy and real brotherhood.

How would we manage our affairs given this attitude?

Our food-producing resources would go much farther if all humans were vegetarian. That's being *practical* because we, on this continent, put far more grain through our animals than we eat ourselves. The world's soil simply could not support the present population if everybody wanted to eat the way Canadians do. It would be impossible. On the other hand, if we were to adopt a vegetarian diet, the existing resources would produce far more wheat, potatoes, corn, soybeans and rice than we could eat.

We hear a good deal about meeting world food needs. A shift in diet is, after all, one of the practical hopes. We don't hear much about it. It wouldn't be popular, and almost a sin, to refuse roast beef. I do think that those who are concerned about feeding the growing population should be thinking about nature of diet. There was a time, of course, when we thought it was impossible to provide a good human nutrition without animal proteins. Today, we know that even soybean meal will furnish *everything* that meat will furnish. There were those who told me, when I adopted vegetarianism, that I would either go back to the old diet or that I would die from malnutrition. Well, about 20 years have gone by and I haven't gone back and I have no fear at all about the next 20 years, if I should live that long.

Do you think mankind's biggest problem, as he is evolving, is one of selfishness?

Oh, I think so. It is in the western world where everybody wants to be rich that the offence has been the greatest. I think humans are basically greedy. I like to read Toynbee. He was an historian who was very pessimistic about the western world. In Toynbee's view, western man must renew his old values and spiritual base or else face the ruin of his civilization.

Why do you not see people doing that?

You do. Toynbee would have said, of course, that two things people in the western hemisphere have to conquer are arrogance and greed. I've become increasingly concerned over the years with human arrogance, greed and cruelty. I don't suppose there is any simple solution to overcome these things, but much of what we can criticize among our fellows is rooted in materialism. I've talked to a lot of kids and have asked them about their aspirations. Their answers usually indicate the making of money. I know there's a conflict between the idea that we are basically greedy and the idea that we are losing our vigour, our punch and our zest to succeed. But, I don't think there is a conflict. On the surface it may appear that there is. I don't think a person has to be greedy. I don't think a person has to be grasping for fists of dollars in order to maintain his muscle and his ambition, vigour and drive. I would like to think that greed could be knocked on the head, but I hate to think of Canadians or people in the western hemisphere or anywhere losing that muscle, fibre and guts that the pioneers had. And we have. They've been eroded, just like soil can be eroded.

You believe that the absence of real challenges, brings on this erosion?

People must have purpose. I think the pioneer had it. His purpose was to get his homestead broken up and fenced and a house on it, and make it a successful farm. He simply went on from there, effectively in most cases. I do wish that kids today could see more of a challenge and knew where to look for goals. Many young people in grades 11 and 12 have little or no concept about where they're going. They need a purpose and it's up to them to find it. They'll be better citizens in God's community, if they have something to work for—an ideal.

How do you translate this zeal into influencing other people? By example only or by contrivance?

I'm inclined to shrink from debate on my diet. I would just as soon not talk about it but if I'm out at a banquet, I would like it fine if everyone could see what I am eating. I'd like it even better if they approach me on the subject. I'd like to have the opportunity of elaboration. I'm not going to peddle it and I would rather leave my testimony by way of example. I like to be subtle about it. I'm critical of some of the evangelism that we see today. I don't even know if it's proving very effective. I think there is a better way of selling your ideas and I don't intend to take to the stump. That is one of the reasons why I broke with denominationalism. It's also one reason why I broke with party politics. I was a party man at one time and whether the enthusiasm was artificial or not, I displayed it. I think it cost us too much. I don't think it served the highest purpose. I think politics today would be more effective if more politicians were independents and were judged on performance rather than by their party.

How would you behave in parliament given your philosophy? Would you do what you felt was right, or would you act in line with the popular con-census among your constituents?

I don't suppose I would do either completely, but I would hate myself if I buried my own convictions. Personally, I would articulate my personal stand on any issue, but would then try to vote in accordance with my perception of the concensus of the constituency. I think you can come clean. I would admire a politician very much more if he would come out now and again and say, "I don't believe in capital punishment, but the people in my constituency are strongly in support of it and I think there should be a poll taken and that it should be a free vote."

You don't believe in consciously moulding others to think the way you think?

I think if I have a God-given conscience, instinct or body of reason, a just God has given the others exactly the same. It is their opportunity and their duty to make the most of them.

Could you elaborate on your love of history and heritage?

It's a long story and you've heard me say before that the teachers in my public school years did nothing for me history-wise except to make me hate history, and the reason I think was fairly obvious. The only history I got in my school years was English history. There was no such thing as a recorded Canadian history. There was no textbook. The teachers didn't know anything about Canadian history. I got English history until I confess I was fed up with it. Reviewing the names and records of kings didn't appeal to me, and I left school with no love of history.

This changed when I became a little more mature and realized that I was growing up in a community where people around me were so much a part of history, particularly western Canadian history. These were pioneer people. My own parents belonged to a generation which came in soon after the railroad arrived. I knew that they had a story and that there were people around me who made me laugh and inspired me with their stories, but that nothing was happening to record their memories.

I think I possess a strong instinct towards conservation. Some, perhaps, would call it no more than thrift. My mother said that waste was a sin and that thrift was a virtue. Well, I too subscribe to that. Carrying that concept a little further, I saw the records of the Red River Valley Board after the 1950 Winnipeg Flood spending about $30 million to make repairs, and then I discovered that the Winnipeg people had themselves to blame for some of this. They had never considered the possibilty that the Red River had a flood history. They'd ignored that and they'd wait unitl the flood of 1950 to get their dykes in shape. Still, they should check their history if they think they have solved their flood problem. There was an even bigger flood in 1926.

There were lots of floods in Winnipeg that came close to the levels of 1950, but people had taken them for granted and they were far enough apart that each time they occurred, people ignored their implications.

I think the story of our development in western Canada is packed with examples like that. Happily, we're now beginning to realize that history is more than a plaything and a hobby, but that it has a value and a use. I remind my senior friends, now and again when I face some of them, that their voices should be heard more loudly today. I think that Canada is in some trouble. I'm not one of the optimists who think that trouble is going to end in a matter of weeks or months. We may have it for a long time. But the voice of the seniors who know something about the ups and downs, about the troubles of the '30's, about the severity of the depression of that time, have a better realization that what took place before can happen again.

I wish there were a few seniors in the House of Commons. I wish there were a few seniors in the legislature and a senior or two on the city council. I think that the voice of someone who knows a bit about history could save taxpayers at all levels of government a fair sum. I think of what I heard the Hon. John Diefenbaker say on a public platform. "In my opinion, nobody is qualified to be a candidate for public office at any level of government in Canada until that person knows something of the history of the community or the area he or she would be called upon to administer." He was saying, in effect, that an administrator is in a better position to plan for tomorrow if he knows what happened yesterday. I think that makes sense.

Anyway, this is another step in the development of my personal interest in history. As I found myself becoming more and more involved and doing a little more digging, or research if you like, I found these historical convictions strengthening. I've tried to share that point of view. Indeed, Canadians, and particularly Albertans, have developed a new interest in history, while they might have scorned the study 50 years ago and barely tolerated it 20 years ago.

I think of the record of local histories. As recently as two days ago, I was at a community not far from Calgary where they were announcing the publication of their local history, and they were delighted. I went around to see their first copy sold by auction at $3,200—some indication of local enthusiasm.

Where was this?

At Rosebud. In 1967, our Centennial Year of Confederation, every community was looking for a project. For every community that wanted to build a new library or park, there was a least four that decided to prepare local histories, and this in spite of criticisms that no one would ever take the time to read them. Well, the books were published and they did sell. I think some of them must have been read because the next year, twice as many communities undertook to do the same job and the next year, the number doubled again and doubled again and doubled again, until today, in the historical resources library in Edmonton, there are over 800 titles of local histories written and published in Alberta.

Why are people interested in history? I think it's more than just sentiment.

I think it does reflect a realization that we'd better know something about the way industry or our community developed, or the recurrence of things like the Spanish flu. We should be able to laugh about the fun that grandfather had. We could be better citizens if we knew more about the people who led the way, and broke the trail and gave this area a community.

You're right when you say I wasn't an historian by training. I stumbled into it. It was a long, slow process. But looking back, I can say that history has been a capital companion for me.

Could you tell me a bit more about your interest in historical personalities— whether it be David Thompson or Bob Edwards, or the mountie you wrote about, or Mother Fulham. What is it about personalities that attracts you?

I think that you could teach a course in Canadian history or western Canadian history under a different title—Canadian Personalities or Canadian Biographies. I came close to doing it one year. I did it in part and I think if it was done properly, it would have a strong appeal. After all, history is mostly biography. If you were to take people and horses out of history, there wouldn't be anything left worth talking about. I believe that biography is the best way to inspire young people. Kids need heroes. I've done quite a bit of probing in the form of polls taken on public school students. I've asked this question, "Having regard to your boyhood or your girlhood reading and observations, who has emerged as your hero?" I don't need to tell you now the strange list of personalities who have come to the top. But what impresses me, I have yet to meet the kid who can't give you a name.

I think every child has a hero or a heroine. It might take him just a moment or two to identify that person. They may have a multiplicity of heroes, but it must reflect a need. I think kids need heroes. Heroes are just leading personalities.

What is it in the individual that causes you to say, "Here's a topic for me to write about." What is it that you see or what do you look for?

Well, I think again, I'm not sure there's a perfect parallel between writing subjects and good history, but I think that if you were looking for a good subject for writing and had history in mind, you would have to find somebody who achieved something, wasn't all saint and wasn't all sinner. But a little of both is important.

You've carried on a very, very full life, and your capacity for work seems inexhaustible. Can you tell me a little bit about the driving force that makes you do this?

Well, to be honest, I don't know the answer. I guess I'm pretty fortunate in having inherited a bit from people who had pioneer drive. My father was quite tireless and I never heard my mother say she was tired. And yet she must have been tired lots of times. I think that the first prerequisite, if you were going to present something systematically, is a good strong body. That means, I think, giving some thought to what you eat and the way you eat it, and certainly some thought to constant exercise. I don't think it's good enough to do a big day's work on Saturday and lounge around the television for the rest of the weekend. I think you have to be active and be doing things steadily. I'm not sure whether it will explain what you have in mind or not, but I'm sure that it will pay off in later years.

What about work? Do ever feel like not wanting to do it and say, "Gee, I don't want to do this column tonight."

Oh yes.

Do you ever feel like sitting and doing nothing?

Oh yes. There are times when writing a column is a bit of a burden, but I think the subdiscipline of having to do that column is good to me. It's particularly good to me to think now I have to do it and therefore I guess I can do it. It would be easy to say I can't think of anything to write about so I guess I won't write it. But, by gum, you have to write it. "Alright, we'll write it and we'll come up with something."

But do you ever feel like not doing anything. Today I just feel like sitting around. Do you ever feel that way?

No, no, not yet. It might happen one of these days, I suppose. It would be awful to be caught up so you had nothing left to do. I think I came close to it a few times in my life when I was bored awfully. The worst piece of work I ever did in my life was with the provincial government in Saskatchewan. I was with the Department of Agriculture. They put me in an office and I didn't have enough to do. I sat there at my desk and I drew funny pictures and I watched the clock. That was the worst working experience in my life.

It's nice, I think, to have something to do tomorrow, particularly if it's something that you want to do. It will make it much easier to get up in the morning and get up with a zest. I think about older people today, most of whom are well fed and well clothed and well housed. They *haven't* enough to keep them occupied. You see some of them with their faces pressed against the windowpane when you go by their lodge. They are looking for something to happen and they have nothing to do until comes next meal time. I think it's sad. A person needs a variety of interests, of course.

Do you think variety's important?

Oh, I do indeed. There was a time when boys were told to pick a profession or vocation and stay with it. But I would say, pick a profession or vocation and don't stay with it. Be prepared to move. The chances are that you'll move with new vigour, desire and purpose and the job itself will benefit.

How do you know when to move? Do you think things just happen to propel you in a certain direction or do you think you have to make a conscious move from instinct?

I think everybody gets the chance. They have to have some courage and be ready to gamble. Often changing jobs is risky. You should be prepared to take the risk and even suffer a setback. But I believe that the change of scenery and of responsibility, plus the challenge, will more than pay off.

You've exhibited that in your life, haven't you? You've made some major changes?

Yes, I've made a few changes and if I had my life to live over again, I would *not* want to settle for fewer. I think I'd like to go for more. I had 23 years at university which was a good experience, but I could have had *two* more careers if I had stopped earlier. I think I might have been a richer man—not in dollars, but in experience. I think 23 years was too long to spend at one task. Now a lot of people can stay with one livelihood and still bring in the other avenues of variety.

So you think the work ethic is something that you just had, just developed, and hasn't been something you've had to work on?

I think I've had a pretty good degree of stamina.

You don't get tired?

Yes, I get a little tired but it doesn't really stop me. Well, nowadays I could be a little bit stiff. I did a lot of hoeing yesterday—hoed in the day and hoed at night. I was a little tired last night. It didn't stop me. It was the darkness that ultimately stopped me. But a night of sleep, happily, at my age, seems to revive me.

What about your threshold of pain? You must have a very high threshold of pain because you manage to keep going through adversity where most of us would look for easier alternatives.

I guess I came from a strain of people—I never heard my dad say that he was hurting. I know that there are lots of times when he was hurting a good deal. But it was a bit of a reflection upon a person who admitted that he was sick or hurt. There was some incentive to keep going, to keep your personal troubles to yourself. The rest of the world had plenty of them without adding a few to theirs. I think that would be it.

Grant, I know that your training has been in agriculture and you've written textbooks on agriculture, and you primarily began as a career person in agriculture. Could you tell me a little bit about your beliefs and role in agricultures?

Well, I was born on a farm. The MacEwans did alright farming and made a little money, apparently, and sold out when I was about six years of age and we went to live in the city. We were going to become city people and I started to go to school in the city. Unfortunately, it wasn't very long before we were in trouble. My father had bought quite a bit of city property and the values went down when they were supposed to go up, and we were bankrupt and on our way back to the land with a new realization that perhaps we shouldn't have left it in the first place.

The frontier, in the intervening years, had receded by four or five hundred miles. It happened that my father had bought a piece of land in northern Saskatchewan on speculation with no thought in the world of ever living on it. So, we set out with a carload of settler's effects—mostly household furniture—for the particular location. We were sorry for ourselves because our city standard of living was going to fall, and it did fall, awfully fast. But, in spite of having a little sympathy for ourselves, we discovered before very long, it was the best thing that could have happened. We were back on the land. We were on good land and we were farming with the new purpose of perpetuity. I didn't stay on the farm but I had a brother who intended to stay on the farm. He died too early to be a farmer. I've never lost my fondness for the land. I think today my first loyalty is to the soil.

You're right, I was trained in agriculture, and there was a time when I thought I had all the answers in the area in which I was working. I was at the University of Saskatchewan for 23 years in the Faculty of Agriculture.

I wrote a few textbooks, but there was nothing that will convince me more clearly about how things have changed in agriculture than to pick up one of my own textbooks. They are completely out-of-date except for a few basic principles. They wouldn't help anybody. Agriculture's changed. I haven't kept abreast of it. I'm a back number. I'm out of date. That hasn't affected my loyalty. It hasn't changed my affection. If I were looking for another vocation, and I thought I had the years to justify it, I'd be going back to the land. I'd be going back to farm, but not necessarily the way they're farming today because that way of farming doesn't appeal to me anymore.

The agriculture I like to think about is the old family farm where you diversified. You had a number of crops of different kinds and you had enough to keep you busy the year 'round. Everybody in the family was involved. The farm wasn't awfully big, but it wasn't necessarily awfully small. Nobody on those farms became wealthy, but you couldn't starve them out. And there were some compensations. The school, church, community hall and curling rink brought the rural people together as much as time would allow amid genuine fellowship. I think that the people at the period whistled more and conversed more and laughed more. They made their own fun. They made their own stories. Oh, I kick myself that I didn't start early to gather up some of those homespun stories that were related maybe at the livery stable, at church, or by farmers at their line fence. And they were homegrown.

They are neither sexy nor obscene. They were enough, however, to make people laugh and laugh hilariously. They were great. I think there was more real humour than the stories that are told today.

And if we digress a bit, humour is very important in your life. You have a delightful sense of humour. You firmly believe in the value of good humour, don't you?

Well, I don't know if I have or not, but I like to see the people indulging in genuine humour and I think that we've seen humour deteriorate seriously in the United States and in Canada. I don't know where you'd go find a Will Rogers today, or a Stephen Leacock or a Bob Edwards or a Haliburton. These people are great. Their stories were the kind that could be told anywhere, with the possible exception of Bob Edwards'. Bob Edwards departed a little bit and he wrote a few stories that wouldn't sound too well in the parlours of that time. He was somewhat ostracized because of that. Generally, the humour was rich. It wasn't cut and dried and catalogued. There were not professional humorists. There was nobody on the radio or television who was called a humorist and therefore felt he had to live up to it by hiring research workers to gather stories and put them on index cards. Will Rogers didn't follow a script. It was spontaneous.

So, spontaneity and wit are two of the factors that you see as being possessed by agricultural people as you remember?

I think yes. Even today's rural people have lost a lot because they're not as close to the soil anymore. When they lived on the soil, if there was any magic about the soil, they benefitted by it. The day before yesterday when I was in southern Alberta, I started counting the derelict and abandoned homes. This is partly because many farmers today are living in the city.

Does that upset you?

Yes, it does. It bothers me. I think we've lost something that helped to make western Canada distinctive and great. Maybe it'll never come back.

If I had the choice, I'd probably select the same parents and I'd want to be born on a farm. Well, I'd live the simple life, struggle a little bit to get my education and I guess I'd ultimately marry the same and have the same child, and same son-in-law and the same grandchildren. I don't know how I could improve on that very much. I would certainly aim for the same degree of variety or more, and I might dedicate myself to a few of my convictions earlier. But I can't complain about that. I had to find them, I had to discover them and because it wasn't part of an early plan, but part of an evolution, I think it has meant more to me.

Tell me about thrift. Does your concept of thrift link with your idea of purpose and conservation?

Yes, I think good conservation is good thrift. I think good thrift is good conservation. Thrift is something that is bred in people who haven't had it too easy. I think it's much easier for the person who's a little bit hungry to be thrifty than the one who's never known what it was to be short of food. A big part of the world's population today must be thrifty. It's enforced thrift. I think all the more that those of us who have had good fortune should be thrifty by conviction. Unhappily, today's society seems self-satisfied rather than thrifty. We're satisfied to use tomorrow's resources. Let the children and the grandchildren and the great-grandchildren worry for themselves.

The United States and Canada are about together in this. The Americans have a $200 billion deficit. They can't come within $200 billion of balancing their budget. I think it's shameful. The Canadian situation is a little worse because on a per capita basis, the deficit, as it was promised to us today, indicates somthing a little higher than the American deficit. I suppose we can survive that. What is worrying me is the fact that nobody seems to care! I don't think the Prime Minister is greatly concerned. I don't hear anybody in the House of Commons saying a lot about the moral obligation to a generation ahead. I think it's nothing short of a shame and a sin to be charging our present high standard of living to the people who are to come later and will not have the oil wells to draw upon. They may have something else but that's problematic. They may find it extremely difficult to have anything kind to say about my generation. If they feel that they should have a share of the oil and the gas, and they see the soil having deteriorated, the waters polluted, the air a mess, the forests run-down, they indeed will have the right to be angry.

Grant, it would appear to me that you're a person who has had a whole host of acquaintances. Yet, you don't appear to consciously cultivate close personal relationships. Is that true?

I think so. It's partly, I suppose, a necessity because of the way I live. I enjoy people but if I'm spending too much time with them, I'm thinking of some things I'd like to get done and are not being done. And you can't be fraternizing socially with your friends and getting these chores done at the same time. It's one or the other. I've got chores. I've got more chores than I'm going to complete in my lifetime. I don't know what they may be but I have the urge to see more of them completed.

Tell me about your interest in ancestral heritage. You've managed to trace your ancestry fairly well. Is this just a sense of history, just a natural interest, and do you think more people should be doing this?

I think my interest in family heritage is akin to my interest in history. Family history is important. Maybe it's not politically important as other varieties of history, but it can be a delightful thing. I think people need something of which they can be proud. Most people can be proud of their heritage—

whether their great-grandparents were saints or scoundrels. Through time, one can develop a sense of admiration for one's forebearers, even if some had less than perfect reputation. "Breathes there the man with soul so dead who never to himself has said, 'This is my own.' " This quote could be referring to a native land, but it could also be about heritage, or family, or something that's worthy of pride. I think it's important to the individual and to the community.

Yes, my own family presented some sources that were of very good interest to me, particularly on my mother's side. The MacEwans, on my father's side, may have had more that they wanted to forget, I don't know. But they didn't leave a very complete record of what transpired. There were a few legends that came down. There was a hint that my great, great grandmother on my father's side was a highland gypsy queen. Some of my relations thought that was nothing to be proud of. I don't know why. I thought that was great. Nobody ever heard about her husband's name or if she had a husband.

But on my mother's side, they were so careful about documenting the story. Why, I don't know, but they did maintain the records. They were on Canadian soil for 210 years, dating to 1773 when they came on the ship "Hector," an old tub that probably had no right to be on the high seas, and I think the ship was 77 days in crossing the ocean. In 1932, I was on a ship for 14 days crossing. It was a freight boat and I thought it was a pretty boring period in my life. Fourteen days seemed like 14 weeks to me, but these people were on for 11 weeks and they lost 17 or 18 people, buried at sea. It was a grim experience. They were coming out at that rather sad time in British history when the peasant folk in the highlands of Scotland were being pushed off the land. The poor soil was not producing enough to maintain a crofter family and leave a little for the landlord. The solution was to convert the land to sheep runs or deer pastures and these people had no place to go. The Grants and the Frasers were among those who were fleeing to some place that would offer opportunity. Their ship was the first to bring Scottish settlers to Pictou Harbour, Nova Scotia.

My mother represented the fifth generation. I'm the sixth generation. Your children are the eighth generation on Canadian soil. I think that calls for a little pride. I think a person would be open to very severe criticism if he allowed that story to be lost.

Grant, why don't you write your autobiography?

Well, I've never said I wouldn't and yet, I agree, I've been slow to accept a few proposals that have been made about writing it. There have been a few reasons. One was that a good friend, Rusty Macdonald, wrote my biography. I think, when considering what he had to work with, that he did an awfully good job. Having seen that come to fulfillment, I could see less point in duplicating even a portion of it by writing my own story. Maybe the day will come when I'll change my mind about that. Another reason is that I've encountered names of people who, in my opinion, would make a better story than my own life would. One will come off the press pretty soon now on Jack Morton, a rather notorious fellow in some ways, but one I think who had qualities that lend themselves more to biography than I think you'd find in my life. Beyond that, I think if there's anything to be written about me, I'd prefer somebody else wrote it rather than write it myself.

Grant, what do you plan to do with the next ten, twenty years? The way you're going now, I think that's a fair question.

I'm not presuming I'll be around ten or twenty years from now, but if I am, there are a few things I'd like to do and I hope that God will give me the muscle and the strength to do them. I think, if I am able, I will continue to write. I'm not presuming that anybody will want to read the stuff that I will write, but that won't stop me. I have to be busy. I see more to write about now than I did when I started. It's also a great pastime. I said that writing had been my companion. I think it's a companion that will last. I enjoy doing the digging and the research that goes with writing. It might be that I will be a little handicapped at the age of 90 or 100 to do the things I would like to do by way of research, but there's some I'd like to do.

I'd like to pursue my almost spiritual interest in soil. I think that God made man out of soil. He made provision of course, to make soil out of man, and I think the two go together. One of the tragedies of our time is the degree of deterioration that's taking place in our soils. We should be more conscious of this loss because it has been with us for so long. It happened in ancient days and it happened in the Land of Milk and Honey when the Israelites were on their way to the Promised Land. It's happened so often, certainly I've had a glimpse of it. I'd like to spend more time investigating and taking pictures of some of these eroded scenes, and writing stories about the degree of loss and bringing them back home to Canada, and scaring the heck out of Canadians. I don't know if I could do it or not.

I'd also like to put a pack on my back and tramp the International Boundary. I think that there's a story there that hasn't been written and which should be. It might do something for American and Canadian relations, not just to capture the politics of the boundary but to capture the human interest side. For example, the stories about people whose house was on the border—the front door was in the United States, back door in Canada; the people who indulged in rum running across that boundary. The stories are rich. It would be fun, I think, to start gathering them up. Not just for the laughs, but I think Canada has a debt to the United States. We don't often recognize it. I'd like to do it as a dedication to good neighbours.

The Workers
by Max Foran

The cool, blue mist of morning was gone from the valley of the Little Red Deer River, and now the hot August sun blazed high in the sky. Grasshoppers clicked in the waving meadow that swept from the river to the half-completed log cabin at the top of the ridge. Here the grey-haired figure bent low over a cedar log, stripping the bark with an old drawknife. If he felt the heat he gave no sign. The sweeps of the drawknife were long and purposeful. Aromatic chips flew in the air until the pale beauty of the inner log was revealed. Only then did the man straighten and wipe his brow with his arm.

Perspiration and blood from a cut wrist stained his faded brown shirt. He bent again to grasp the heavy log, ignoring the nagging pain from a damaged vertebrae. The doctor had advised him to do no lifting. But he had little time for medical men. They pampered the body and made guesses based on vaguely conceived norms. For him, his own norms were equally valid. A combination of inveterate optimism and determination told him that two logs were going to sit in position six feet off the ground, notched and snug, before his driver came for him at 6:00 p.m.

Slowly he lifted the 250-pound end and dragged it into position. A blunt pencil appeared from the pocket of aged, baggy trousers, and in a few minutes the log was marked, ready for notching. Whistling tunelessly, he strode past the jumbled pile of unused logs to the tree where his axe rested beside the jam sandwich that he would eat for lunch—if he remembered, or if he had the time.

Time! This was the key to his urgency, here today and to everything he did. His time was not rooted in instinctive reactions to seasonal change, nor did it harbour the spectre of death or incapacitation, for like all of his kind, he accepted his seeming indestructability. No, his actions were determined by deadlines of the clock. He would leave this place at 6:00 p.m. only because another task had priority by the clock. He would return, not when his instincts moved him nor when he desired, but when he could slot it in between the man-made hands of time. The pale blue eyes looked skyward, following a lone duck as it rose above the aspens, head thrust southwards. So much alike, man and beast . . . always time to do, or to go.

He bent to his axe. He loved few things, admired fewer and valued hardly any. But he liked a good axe. Its utility lay in its keenness and in the hand and eye of the wielder. He stood over the cedar log and rhythmically he began to chop the short, sure strokes of the expert. The sounds echoed across the meadow, down to the gurgling stream and along the high banks touching the ears of the little furry creature who, too, was bent at a task of his own.

The waters of the Little Red Deer River are placid but never quiet in the green season. They ripple over the shoals and cascade gently over half-submerged logs and stones. The whirring of the water beetles and the heavy scent of clover helped lull the senses on this still August day. On the bank, a small salamander lay sunning himself, while a hot robin sought a cooling bath at the water's edge. If the old beaver felt the heat he gave no sign.

Hunched back on his tripod of webbed back legs and flat tail, he methodically worked his way through the last fibres holding up a stubborn aspen poplar. The tree fell at last, just missing the beaver who was slow to jump aside because of his partially crushed hind leg. For a moment he stood erect, blunt muzzle inquisitively searching the air. One eye was closed, a painful legacy to a sharp twig three years previously.

Presently, the beaver limped over to the fallen aspen and began cutting it up. For a long time he gnawed away at the choice branches that would feed his young in the winter. Was it instinct or intelligence which told the usually nocturnal creature that he should break habit and work during the day? An accident of Nature or an act of Man had partially destroyed his dam, and now he must hurry to complete it before the russet days turned to white; before the rippling waters became mute victims of winter's grip. Painfully and laboriously he dragged the logs one by one to the river bank. Then he was in the water and his movements were transformed into graceful symmetry. By mid-afternoon, the cut-up pieces were in position, wedged into the dam or imbedded in the soft mud at the river's bottom. With the hot rays of the sun on his fur, he pulled himself out of the water and crawled onto the bank. Then, with his injured leg dragging, he made his way to a tall aspen and began to gnaw at its thick trunk.

He used the heavy crowbar carefully, turning the log over as he balanced precariously on a homemade sawhorse. Slowly, the heavy log turned under the leverage and with a dull thud fell into its notched space. He examined the fit closely. Satisfied, he fetched a plastic cup and filled it with spring water from a dented Javex bottle. He drank thankfully, not deeply but with relish, his solitary toast to success. He did not sit, but moved constantly. His back ached and the grey pallor of fatigue haunted the lined features. By the tree the jam sandwich lay bleeding hotly in a pastic bag.

Six times he had moved the two logs in and out of position. Six times the axe blade hewed and shaped the notches until they were moulded and smooth. Alone, he had hoisted and manoeuvred the 20 foot logs six feet off the ground. Scattered uselessly on the dirt were the four cedar butts that he had buck-sawed from the ends. Slivers were imbedded in his hands while a pinched thumb began to throb. He ignored both and glanced at his watch. Five-thirty. Time enough to go to the river's edge and retrieve the beaver log he had seen the week previously.

Hitching up his trousers and tightening the tie which he used for a belt, he clambered down the hill, through the fireweed and wild asters to the river's edge. He found the sodden branch lying on the bank, a dull brown slab of anonymity that would come alive under his carving knife. As he examined the log's smooth wetness, the serrated edges of the beaver's teeth gleamed back at him. He had just tucked the log under his arm, and was about to grab a handhold on a willow branch to haul himself to the top of the bank when he saw the beaver.

The man crouched beside the willow bush and observed the beaver's dexterity and doggedness as it guided a poplar branch to the water's edge. He was not close enough to notice the limp or, of course, the eye, and he would have been surprised, maybe incredulous, had he been told that the beaver, contrary to habit, had worked all day in the hot sun. For the beaver was tired. Fatigue was there in his flagging movements and in his lack of vigilance which should have alerted him of the human presence 40 yards away. But the man could not tell this. It was hidden from him as were truths about his own condition hidden from others.

He had a special affinity with the beaver. To him the beaver was the natural sublimation of a lifestyle he sought to cultivate. It worked patiently and with method. It harmed no fellow creature, and took nothing it did not earn and used everything it took. It was in harmony with Nature and had developed instincts and abilities which made it efficient and durable in a harsh environment. He was not a religious man in the orthodox sense, but he believed in a Supreme Being and in Nature as the unfolding of a Divine Plan. His theology combined Protestanism and Pantheism, and in this respect the beaver symbolized the fusion of both. After 15 minutes, the man rose and turned up the hill. His failing ears did not hear the slap of tail on water as the beaver, disturbed at last, headed for haven. He did not look back, for his mind was already on other things as he took the shortest and steepest route up the incline. At the top of the hill he changed into an outmoded suit complete with frayed shirt and shapeless tie. His eyes did not dwell on the beautiful mellowing blend of spruce and sky to the west. Instead he picked up a shovel and headed for his garden. He was digging in the potato patch when the black car drove up.

Dust hung in the air as the Chrysler Imperial swooped down the narrow dirt road, past Eagle Hill, heading away from the sun and to another world. Contrary to protocol, he sat in the front seat. He did not approve of the car, anyway. Its "quiet elegance" and luxury appalled his sense of frugality and conservation. Like many things in modern man's inventory of needs, it was very much a misplaced overstatement. The C.B.C. news was blaring its account of human strife in a sad and sorry world when he noticed a red-tailed hawk sitting on a fence post, a gopher dangling limply from its talons. In his reflective mood, the contrast was not lost on him: Mankind's rational depredations and Nature's pitiless harmony. He found his own ethic, not in redressing the former but in becoming part of the latter, using his humanity to modify the "pitiless." For he could choose, whereas his friend the hawk could not.

He pulled a notebook from his pocket and began to write. He was speaking at 8:00 p.m. to a group at Calmar, and his topic, "Western Characters I Have Known" needed some thought. He jotted them down one by one as they came to mind: Frederick Haultain, Jimmy Gardiner, Chief Walking Buffalo, Billy Henry, Walter Murray, that old Manitoba Mountie turned poet, the Calgary second-hand dealer who was collecting information on East Calgary buildings, the grizzled farmer from Melfort who used to take his prize pigs to town in the back seat of his new Packard, the old lady from Grouard who cared for every stray creature she found . . . . There were so many. He wrote steadily in his small compact writing until the Hobbema turn-off when he put his notebook back in his pocket. For a few minutes he stared vacantly at the ribbon or road stretching straight ahead. Then the grey head drooped forward.

Darkness came quickly and suddenly at the river. It crept over the hills, folded under the spruce stands and piled up in the marshy recesses. Throughout the night the beaver worked, not stopping to rest. Around midnight his attention shifted from logs to chinking. He was in his lodge stuffing mud into the spaces when the first rays of morning light shafted through the conical tunnel at the top of the lodge. Instinctively the beaver moved down to his platform just above the water level. He lay down and rested his head on his outstretched front paws. The one eye fluttered shut and he slept.

They rested fitfully as if rebelling against sleep's languid embrace. They almost seemed to will wakening and a reunion with the tasks to which they were both bound. For they are the workers.

◆◆◆◆◆

MacEwan skating, December 12, 1969. Photo credit to Provincial Archives of Alberta.